VGM Opportunities Series

OPPORTUNITIES IN
OSTEOPATHIC
MEDICINE
CAREERS

Terence J. Sacks

Foreword by
John B. Crosby, J.D.
American Osteopathic Association

 **VGM Career Books**
NTC/Contemporary Publishing Group

331.7
S 121

Library of Congress Cataloging-in-Publication Data

Sacks, Terence J.
    Opportunities in osteopathic medicine careers / Terence J. Sacks
        p.   cm. — (VGM opportunities series)
    ISBN 0-658-00184-1 (cloth) — ISBN 0-658-00186-8 (pbk.)
    1. Osteopathic medicine—Vocational guidance. I. Title. II. Series.

RZ341 .S23 2000
615.5'33'023—dc21

00-44215

Published by VGM Career Books
A division of NTC/Contemporary Publishing Group, Inc.
4255 West Touhy Avenue, Lincolnwood (Chicago), Illinois 60712-1975 U.S.A.
Copyright © 2001 by NTC/Contemporary Publishing Group, Inc.
Printed in the United States of America
International Standard Book Number: 0-658-00184-1 (cloth)
                                                        0-658-00186-8 (paper)

01   02   03   04   05   06   LB   15   14   13   12   11   10   9   8   7   6   5   4   3   2

DEDICATION

This book is dedicated to my wife, Mary Jane, my most loyal and constant companion, whose unceasing support and good counsel have given me the push needed to complete this book.

Her wise advice whenever I ran into a blind alley and her encouragement in following up on messages and assignments have been absolutely essential in completing this book. Her understanding of the necessity of giving priority to this and other similar assignments has served to make my load ever so much lighter. Truly, I owe to her whatever success this book may have.

CONTENTS

Growth of osteopathic medicine. Achievements in the field. Results of studies. Places to work. Training. An alternative to traditional medicine. Selecting a school. Conclusion.

Colonial medicine. Initiating change. Two schools of medicine. Establishing a new school. The birth of the association. A challenge to the profession. Growth in the profession.

Profiles of some practicing doctors of osteopathic medicine. Complementing medical science—OMT. Treating the patient. Salaries for doctors of osteopathic medicine.

ABOUT THE AUTHOR

Terence J. Sacks is an independent writer-editor with more than twenty-five years' experience in communications. During that period he has written dozens of news stories, magazine articles, and speeches. Sacks's articles have appeared in such publications as *Hospitals* and *Chicago Medicine.*

Sacks, a graduate of Northwestern University's Medill School of Journalism, has strong credentials in the field of health care. For three years, from 1970 through 1973, he was director of communications for the Chicago Medical Society, the local professional group for physicians in Chicago and Cook County. He has also held positions in communications for the American Osteopathic Association, the American Association of Dental Schools, and for several hospitals in Chicago.

Sacks is currently on the journalism faculty of Columbia College in Chicago, where he teaches "Introduction to the Mass Media." At Columbia he has also taught courses in news reporting, feature writing, editing company publications, and the history of journalism.

For more than a decade, Sacks has headed his own writing and communications firm, Terence J. Sacks Associates. He is active in the Independent Writers of Chicago (where he served on the board), the American Medical Writers Association, and the Publicity Club of Chicago.

FOREWORD

Congratulations! You are about to discover the world of osteopathic medicine, one of the best-kept secrets in American health care. Though osteopathic principles and practices date back to the mid-1800s, very few Americans understand the important role that osteopathic physicians have played in influencing modern medicine. This book is designed to explain the origins of this distinctive profession and to reveal the fulfilling career path offered as a doctor of osteopathic medicine (D.O.).

When Andrew Taylor Still, M.D., first founded the osteopathic medical profession, many of his contemporaries were skeptical of his philosophies. Dr. Still's "whole person" approach to medicine was simply unheard of by other medical doctors of his day, many of whom relied on amputation, purgatives, and heavy narcotics to treat illnesses. Despite these criticisms, Dr. Still was determined to provide a higher standard of patient care. He sought to minimize invasive procedures, to enhance the body's ability to heal itself, and to teach doctors and patients alike that good health is about more than the absence of disease.

Today, osteopathic medicine is the fastest growing healthcare profession in the United States. There are more than 4,000 osteopathic physicians practicing in every state and in every medical specialty area. All D.O.s are fully trained and licensed physicians, just like M.D.s. In fact, many M.D.s and D.O.s practice side by side. Though osteopathic physicians are still a minority in the total physician workforce, D.O.s (more than half of which specialize in primary care) have filled an important niche in health care, particularly for rural and other medically underserved communities.

Osteopathic medicine has withstood its share of challenges over the years, but its ideals have passed the test of time. As osteopathic physicians receive 100 million patient visits per year, it is clear that there is something important about the distinctive care that D.O.s provide. Perhaps after reading this book, you too will understand the D.O. difference.

John B. Crosby, J.D.
Executive Director
American Osteopathic Association

ACKNOWLEDGMENTS

Obviously, it takes the encouragement and the contribution of many to complete a book such as this. For one, I would like to acknowledge the invaluable assistance I received from Karyn Gianfrancesco, external communications manager of the American Osteopathic Society and Cathy Kearns, director of communications and member services of the American Association of Colleges of Osteopathic Medicine. Both were most kind in supplying materials of inestimable value in completing this assignment. Also, Ms. Julie Rosenthal, director of admissions at the Chicago College of Osteopathic Medicine, who was most generous of her time in explaining the admissions procedure at her college. Also extremely helpful was Ms. Candace Passi, dean of students at the Chicago College of Osteopathic Medicine.

I am especially grateful for the kind assistance and time of those who consented to being interviewed and whose comments are interspersed throughout the book. These include Dr. Cliff Ireland of Skokie, Illinois, Dr. David Zeiger of Chicago, Dr. Patricia Roy of Muskegon, Michigan, Dr. Tyler

Cymet of Baltimore, Dr. Keith Glaws of Winnetka, Illinois, Dr. Karen Nichols of Mesa, Arizona, and Dr. David Abend of Emerson, New Jersey. I should not omit the generous time and help given by the reference staff at the Skokie Public Library. Finally, I must acknowledge the many kind suggestions and comments of my editors at NTC/Contemporary Publishing Group. Their comments helped make the book more readable and meaningful.

INTRODUCTION

Throughout its history, osteopathy has been reviled by some as quackery, chicanery, or even worse, as a cultist sham. Nothing could be further from the truth. In fact, osteopathy is a rational system of medical care that is formulated on the belief that all systems of the body are interrelated, and that what affects one part of the body will have corresponding effects on other parts of the body. Therefore, the whole person, including emotional state as well as overall physical condition, must be considered when providing treatment.

Osteopathic medicine originated in the late 1800s with Dr. Andrew Taylor Still who, while treating soldiers, became increasingly disillusioned with the medical practices and techniques of the day. Why? Because, to his mind, they just weren't working.

Dr. Still believed that problems with the musculoskeletal system could affect the nerves and circulatory system that radiate to various organs of the body; thus the true source of many diseases was not actually in the organs themselves, but in the spine, muscles, and joints. Still called these problems "osteopathic." *Osteo* for bone, and *pathic* for disease. He devised OMT—osteopathic manipulation therapy—to break up obstructions in the circulatory system, which enabled the blood to flow naturally and the nerves to function normally. Once the body was in proper balance, it could resume its natural healing processes.

From that time, osteopathic and allopathic medicine, for the most part, remained in separate camps. But by the 1940s, osteopathy gradually began growing in stature and numbers. So much so that today, many people who are dissatisfied with traditional medicine turn to osteopathy, which emphasizes manipulation, nutrition, and a healthy lifestyle over drugs and surgery. Osteopathy makes sense to them, and they like the results they see.

There are many similarities between traditional physicians and doctors of osteopathy. Both must go through years of rigorous medical training. Both must complete a required residency. Both must pass state licensing exams. And, if desired, both must complete an additional two to six years of training in a specialty, although the majority of D.O.s go into family practice. There it ends for the allopathic physician. But the osteopathic physician must receive additional "hands-on" training in osteopathic diagnosis and in OMT.

Today osteopathy enjoys a hard-won and well-deserved reputation as a respectable and rational method of medical treatment. More and more people are realizing the wisdom of a more holistic approach to treating the body, and they are seeking it. Also, the lines separating the allopathic and osteopathic camps are beginning to blur. As this trend continues, it will be beneficial not only for those who are in need of treatment, but for those who provide it as well.

CHAPTER 1

A PROFESSION ON THE RISE

If you had been a doctor in practice in the mid-1950s, you might have read an article in the September 1955 issue of *Medical Economics* that proclaimed in bold letters *"Why Osteopathy is Considered a Cult."* Among other things, the article defined many of the issues that divided osteopathy, then about eighty years old, from the predominant branch of allopathic medicine and the medical doctors who practiced it. Since that time, osteopathic medicine has grown as a profession and has come to be viewed not as a cult but as a respected and effective method of health care delivery.

GROWTH OF OSTEOPATHIC MEDICINE

Professional growth of doctors of osteopathic medicine has been dramatic. You will find it interesting to learn some of the facts that attest to the sharp growth of the osteopathic profession in recent years:

- The number of doctors of osteopathic medicine doubled from 1970 to 1990; the number of medical doctors increased by 84 percent.
- Doctors of osteopathic medicine opened their 19th school in 1998; medical doctors closed their 126th school in 1990.
- Although still the smallest branch of medicine by far with thirty-five thousand active practitioners, doctors of osteopathic medicine are more likely to practice in rural areas and are clustered largely in states with large doctors of osteopathic medicine populations, such as Michigan, Ohio, Pennsylvania, New Jersey, Texas, and Florida.
- Two-thirds of all doctors of osteopathic medicine are primary care physicians, compared to one-third of medical doctors.
- Doctors of osteopathic medicine accept and integrate mainstream medicine into their own program, which includes osteopathic manipulative therapy and other osteopathic concepts.
- Many hospitals that employ doctors of osteopathic medicine have merged with medical doctors' hospitals, and an estimated two-thirds of all doctor of osteopathic medicine graduates enter medical doctors' residencies.

The profession of osteopathic medicine has in recent times tended to move closer to allopathic medicine. The factor of greatest importance in the trend to team the two professions is that both medical doctors and doctors of osteopathic medicine are physicians. Doctors of osteopathic medicine, just like medical doctors, are licensed to prescribe drugs and they can admit patients to hospitals and utilize all available modalities or treatment methods available to medical science. No other health-care providers can make this claim.

It is interesting to note that in recent years all but two state societies of the American Medical Association have accepted doctors of osteopathic medicine as members. Not forgetting the article title that opened this chapter, back in the 1950s many of the members of the association probably labeled them as cultists.

ACHIEVEMENTS IN THE FIELD

Osteopathic medicine can claim other achievements that prove its rapidly emerging status as a healing profession that offers the public something unique and that many people are seeking.

Dr. Michael J. Bradley became the first doctor of osteopathic medicine to be elected president of the Delaware

Medical Society. And the American Academy of Family Physicians, which did not admit doctors of osteopathic medicine as members until 1993, now has 3,383 members who are doctors of osteopathic medicine, or 7 percent of the organization's total membership. And 605 of these members have achieved an even higher distinction by going on to become fellows of the academy. To become a fellow, a physician must be a member for six years and attain six hundred hours of continuing medical education (CME).

Then, too, a large and growing part of the public is interested in the physical manipulation of the body, such as osteopathic manipulative treatment (OMT) to achieve proper and pain-free function. A recent Harvard study found that a third of Americans have tried using nontraditional forms of care in recent years, including OMT.

Based on studies of the federal Agency for Health Care Policy for effectiveness of various treatments, OMT and pain relievers seem to be the only forms of treatment found effective for lower back pain among the hundreds of cases studied. OMT, after years of sharing the same reimbursement code with physical therapists and other nonphysicians, now has its own separate reimbursement system. A few medical doctors—though the numbers are still very modest—are enrolling in OMT courses after getting an indication of the effectiveness of the treatments from doctor of osteopathic medicine associates.

RESULTS OF STUDIES

Studies conducted by the American Osteopathic Association have found that:

- 81 percent of Americans believe that not everyone receives good health care
- 75 percent believe that the health-care system has lost its personal touch
- 71 percent believe that health-care costs are rising unnecessarily and are a "rip-off"
- 67 percent believe that the insurance system compels physicians to provide inferior care in order to save costs

In reply to these complaints, the American Osteopathic Association (AOA) contends that doctors of osteopathic medicine offer a system for treating the whole person, not just a symptom or a disease. Further, says the AOA, this philosophy of patient-focused care allows doctors of osteopathic medicine to provide comprehensive health care aimed at making the patient feel well cared for. Doctors of osteopathic medicine also receive special training in the relationship between the body's structure and function and its ability to heal itself.

As to the often heard criticism that the medical establishment is turning out too many physicians, a typical reply by a leader of osteopathic medicine is that of Thomas W.

Allen, provost and dean of Oklahoma State University College of Osteopathic Medicine, who says, "The kind of physician we're graduating—a family doctor with comprehensive training who is willing to practice outside of urban areas—is just the kind of doctor we need today."

While nearly two-thirds of all practicing doctors of osteopathic medicine are in primary care, more than a third, or thirteen thousand, are certified as specializing in areas other than primary care. For these specialists, the American Osteopathic Association maintains its own certification boards in more than twenty specialties from anesthesiology and dermatology to proctology and radiology. In addition, a few of these boards offer certification in such subspecialties as cardiology, gastroenterology, and neonatology.

Also, several American Osteopathic Association certifying boards offer certification in such specialized and in-demand fields as addiction medicine, critical-care medicine, geriatric medicine, and sports medicine. This duplicates to a great extent the number of boards that certify medical doctors in various specialties of medicine.

There is still another factor that plays a big role in the profession's increasing popularity. A far greater percentage of doctors of osteopathic medicine—approximately 5,539—practice in smaller communities of 25,000 to 50,000 people than in larger cities. Although 9,456 M.D.s practice in small communities, outnumbering doctors of osteopathic medicine more than ten to one, the high number of D.O.s is impressive considering that they represent only a small, though growing, faction of the medical community.

PLACES TO WORK

As to where they practice, it can be safely said that doctors of osteopathic medicine work in settings very similar to those of medical doctors. The greatest numbers of physicians in both branches are in private practice, but by no means are all doctors of osteopathic medicine in private practice. Some are in academic medicine, working either as faculty members or as faculty in teaching hospitals, and others are involved in research. Some doctors of osteopathic medicine work for the federal government as public health officers or as physicians in the Department of Veterans Affairs. A large number of doctors of osteopathic medicine serve with the armed forces, both in the United States and overseas.

Yet another increasingly important area of employment for doctors of osteopathic medicine is industrial medicine, where they are hired to prevent illnesses relating to various workplace issues and to treat accidents and illnesses of workers both on the job and as a result of their line of work.

Some doctors of osteopathic medicine work as flight surgeons. Here they study the effects of high-altitude flight on the physical condition of flight personnel. Doctors of osteopathic medicine also may work in the area of nuclear medicine, where they perform tests on patients using radioactive isotopes and other nuclear imaging equipment.

A good summary that attests to the rise in importance and status of osteopathic medicine can be found in a recent address given by U.S. Surgeon General David Satcher, who said, "Osteopaths have served the underserved communities in proportion far greater than their numbers. They make up 5 to 6 percent of doctors, but 15 percent of those who serve underserved communities."

Meet the Director of External Relations
at the American Osteopathic Association

The Director of External Relations at the American Osteopathic Association talks about how that association is dedicated to educating the public about the practice of osteopathy and defines what the doctor of osteopathic medicine is and does.

"One of the most exciting things that we've undertaken in recent years is what we call a Unity Campaign, which is a program to go external to reach consumers and the media and to let them know more about osteopathic medicine.

"We conducted a study in May that included several small focus groups where we spoke directly with consumers. We found out that 89 percent of the public across the country does not know what a doctor of osteopathic medicine is or what a D.O. does. So, we need to get the word out. For one, we sent out news releases to a variety of television stations; we hoped they would do stories on the field of osteopathic medicine. We also conducted media briefings in New York City. For example, we met with a reporter from *Woman's Day* magazine, representatives of *Country Living,* and a reporter from CNN to try to familiarize them with the work of doctors of osteopathic medicine and with the American Osteopathic Association.

"We are also putting out a bimonthly newsletter called *Wellness Watch,* which goes to media across the country. This newsletter condenses articles from our two magazines—*The Journal of the American Osteopathic Association,* and *The Doctors of Osteopathic Medicine*—and digests them for the media or those who don't work directly in the field.

"Doctors of osteopathic medicine are definitely distinct in certain ways from medical doctors, and we are trying to get that concept across to the public. Many people go to their doctor and they have no idea if the doctor is a medical doctor or a doctor of osteopathic medicine. Because health care is changing rapidly, people are more likely to question their doctor if they see that he is a doctor of osteopathic medicine and not a medical doctor. So the consumer must be educated to realize that the D.O. is just as much of a physician as is the medical doctor, the only difference being the training. D.O.s have a different philosophy of health care than M.D.s. They work with the whole person and they are trained in osteopathic manipulative treatment.

"We conducted a managed care survey last year and about 70 percent of those D.O.s polled replied that they practice OMT (osteopathic manipulative treatment). Perhaps not every day, but they do use it.

"More of the younger D.O.s are impassioned about OMT. A doctor who works with osteopathic medical students called me last week and said that the students all want to know more about OMT and be trained in it so that they can use it later in their own practices.

"In the past there may have been a tendency on the part of some doctors of osteopathic medicine to forget about their osteopathic roots and try to be more accepted as physicians, period—the same as medical doctors. Today, however, many of the older doctors of osteopathic medicine are very proud of their background and what the profession stands for.

"Through education we are informing the public about the field so that we can eliminate the stigma that sometimes was attached to the profession, where the consumer may have thought: 'Well, you're not a real doctor, or you don't have the education that a medical doctor has achieved.' This is not true because the requirements, qualifications, skills taught, and length of the program are exactly the same, except that the doctors of osteopathic medicine receive additional training in OMT.

"And there were some people who thought of D.O.s as doctors who were unable to get into medical school, but that, too, has changed in recent years. Today, the ratio of applicants for enrollment spots in osteopathic medical schools is about four to one, which is considerably higher than the ratio for medical school applicants—about three to one.

"More and more students are going into osteopathic medicine. You see great growth in the number of osteopathic colleges, which is now up to nineteen, and in the total number of osteopathic physicians, now more than forty-three thousand—perhaps even closer to forty-five thousand.

"A few years back we projected that there would be about forty-two thousand doctors of osteopathic medicine by 2020, and we have already surpassed that number, so the profession is growing faster than most people anticipated.

"The rapid growth in the number of D.O.s practicing today reflects the fact that more people are becoming aware of the field of osteopathic medicine and that medical students are recognizing the different, often higher, standards of care in osteopathic medicine. This is combined with the willingness of doctors of osteopathic medicine to practice in rural areas.

"We know that 15 percent of all doctors of osteopathic medicine practice in towns of ten thousand or fewer—that's a pretty healthy percentage of the forty-three thousand doctors of osteopathic medicine in all. A lot of this is based on the fact that 54 percent, more than half of all doctors of osteopathic medicine, practice primary care medicine. This focus on primary care combined with their commitment to practice in underserved populations in rural areas and in the inner city, where there are serious physician shortages, make D.O.s valuable providers of quality medical care in the United States. We opened our newest school in Pikeville, Kentucky, because there is a severe need for doctors in that area.

"As to the osteopathic colleges, there is always the possibility of having several more in the future, but this depends on the individual states. Each state has to decide if it wants a new osteopathic college, and if so, it must discuss this with the American Osteopathic Association to see if the new school can be accredited.

"We always say that doctors of osteopathic medicine are primary care physicians first and specialists second. When D.O.s start their rotating internship after they finish osteopathic college—something medical doctors do not do—they rotate through the primary care areas. After that, they can specialize if they want to, but many are sold on primary care after they do their internships.

"In the past, AOA students had to accept allopathic residencies because there simply were not enough residencies to fill the need. But today we're making a determined effort to increase the number of AOA residencies available to AOA students who want to specialize.

"We estimate that 70 percent of our members belong to the AOA, as compared to about 35 percent of the medical doctors who belong to the AMA. There are several reasons for this. For one, in order to be board certified as a D.O., you have to be a member of the AOA. Also, there is more dissension with student groups in the AMA as compared with our students, most of whom belong to the AOA as student members.

"There has been talk of a merger between the two branches of medicine, but this is something that we feel would not be in the best interest of the profession. The degree of doctor of osteopathic medicine is distinctive, and if the American Osteopathic Association joined the American Medical Association, this distinction would largely be lost. We feel that this distinction needs to be accentuated and not drowned out through a merger. Hopefully the Unity Campaign will make people more educated about the D.O. and his or her work."

Meet a D.O. Practicing Internal Medicine
in Baltimore, Maryland

A doctor of osteopathy describes how osteopathic manipulative therapy can be used to help patients with various ailments.

"We are looking for a change. We are seeking to identify a problem and then to resolve it. We are looking at which area is a problem and what's going on with it. And then we are looking to treat that with some sort of manipulation.

"Many patients come to my office because they are looking for osteopathic manipulation. But it is just one therapeutic modality. It's not something that every single patient receives every single time. I'd say that only about 20 percent of my patients receive some sort of manipulation. It is most applicable in cases where patients have a restricted range of motion; where they are unable to move about as well as they could before. It could be a limitation in their ability to use their arms or legs or spine and in cases where their motion is not what it should be, based on physiology.

"Often weakness in the use of their limbs is some symptom that people are developing osteoarthritis, particularly if it's weakness of the quadriceps, so the manipulation can be used to prevent osteoarthritis or delay the progression of the disease.

"All doctors of osteopathic medicine receive training in osteopathic manipulative therapy (OMT), which is the therapeutic application of force or pressure to a person in order to get a therapeutic result. It differs from a massage, where you are simply applying force without any special attention being paid to where the application of the force would be most therapeutic.

"Pregnant women, for example, will experience many changes in the musculoskeletal system resulting in a lot of aches and pains. Osteopathic manipulation can be used to help free up motion and make a woman feel better. Perhaps the most common use of OMT is on those patients who suffer from lower back pain.

"In the case of a heart attack victim, there are musculoskeletal pains associated with this. People who have had a heart attack usually experience changes in their cervical spine. If we perform OMT on these patients, they will feel better for a day or two, three days at the most, but the core problem has not been addressed. It would not be in keeping with medical science to give a patient osteopathic manipulation until after the reason for heart attack has been treated. What it amounts to is this: We can't completely change a person's anatomy or physiology, but we can remove pressure from body points that cause people pain."

TRAINING

Training courses are essentially the same for medical doctors and doctors of osteopathic medicine. They are both taught by Ph.D.s and cover similar subjects of study. The main difference is really in the philosophy of osteopathic medicine, the specialized training D.O.s receive in OMT and the goals that they set for themselves.

As mentioned earlier, more doctors of osteopathic medicine are beginning to move into the specialties, but the majority still enter primary care—about two-thirds. All of the areas of medical specialties are also open to doctors of osteopathic medicine. In addition, there are specialties in lifestyle medicine and in osteopathic manipulation that are limited to doctors of osteopathic medicine. Lifestyle medicine is a new kind of approach that is concerned with how medicine can enhance people's lives.

Many osteopathic physicians do go into medical doctor controlled residencies. This is due primarily to the fact that others are competing for medical doctors and doctors of osteopathic medicine residencies and sometimes the medical doctor residencies are successful in recruiting the doctors of osteopathic medicine. It's not that there's a lack of residencies for doctors of osteopathic medicine, it's just that when there is a lot of competition for a good product, some people will wind up in medical doctor hospitals and residency training.

AN ALTERNATIVE TO
TRADITIONAL MEDICINE

There is an ever-increasing interest in alternative medicine in treating a range of ailments and illnesses. Common alternative medical practitioners are chiropractors, massage therapists, specialists in herbal medicine, and acupuncturists. More people are turning to alternative medicine as a form of treatment.

Many patients say, "Well, just because you don't have a scientific answer for my problem does not mean that I have to suffer." So the patients are looking elsewhere in many instances. Physicians who do not have all the cures available may also look to alternative treatments.

What these alternative practitioners are doing may not have been proven scientifically, so it may or may not work. But if a doctor has nothing to offer the patient, then he or she should be willing to try so-called alternative approaches to medicine.

Osteopathic medicine will continue to grow numerically in the coming years. There are nineteen osteopathic medical schools now and more applicants than ever. There are now four applicants for every opening in osteopathic school, which is more than the number of applicants to medical school.

In considering osteopathic medicine as a career, you should realize that osteopathic medicine is a small community. Osteopathic physicians are a tightly knit group of providers who rely on each other. Some are trained specialists, but most are generalists who have learned to be comfortable being uncomfortable. They help whenever they can, but if there are matters that they don't know about, they have no problem relying on others who do.

It is debatable whether any of the old hostilities or bitterness between the two branches of medicine are still in effect. Both disciplines are fighting the same battles. D.O.s are fully trained physicians as are medical doctors, in contrast to partially trained providers such as physician assistants, who do not have residency training or postgraduate training and who don't have the breadth of knowledge of a fully trained physician.

So D.O.s are partnering with medical doctors because the issues are pretty similar. Medical doctors are looking to partner with D.O.s because they feel that they need the D.O.'s help. By and large, doctors of osteopathic medicine are accepted in all hospitals. In Maryland, for example, there is not a hospital that will not accept doctors of osteopathic medicine. Right now there are close to three hundred doctors of osteopathic medicine in the state of Maryland—it was about half that number back in the seventies. So the osteopathic physician has increased in stature and prominence here in the last ten or fifteen years.

As to a possible merger of the two branches of medicine, this might happen, speaking truthfully, anywhere between fifty and a hundred years from now. Once both professions become secure with their identities and realize the interrelationship between themselves, the two will merge. But as mentioned before, this won't happen in our lifetime. It will probably take a century to accomplish.

SELECTING A SCHOOL

In choosing an osteopathic college, out of the current nineteen schools in existence, you should know that many of these schools consider the residency of the applicant a prime factor in their operations, though some schools don't. The California School of Osteopathic Medicine, for example, has a strong interest in retaining students from its own state. It is seeking to rebuild its osteopathic ranks since the merger in 1961 of the California Osteopathic Association and the California Medical Association nearly dessimated California's osteopathic community. Students researching osteopathic medical schools should first look at what schools are in their geographic area. Economics also play a major role in choosing a school. You have to consider how much can you afford and what sort of programs the schools offer.

Then there are matters of personal choice. Do you like the area in which the school is located? Do you prefer going to Iowa or to California? Geographic location for at least the next four or five years of your life is a pretty key consideration in choosing a school to attend.

Faculty is another key consideration. Has the faculty been teaching at the school for a long time? Or has there been a large turnover in the faculty over a period of just a few years? You should look for a faculty that is stable, that has been around and has a good reputation.

I strongly recommend that any student who wants to go to osteopathic medical school personally tour the school—that you actually go there and spend a day taking classes, talking to students and faculty, and having lunch with them. Let them know you're interested in the field and ask them about their experiences. Then you can see what it's like for yourself.

Ultimately, it comes down to you, the individual student. How much effort do you intend to put into your studies? When you go to medical school, your whole life changes. It's never going to be same after that.

Medicine is more intense than law school; it's more intense than college. The volume of information that you are exposed to is enormous, but it's a tremendous experience that offers a chance to grow personally as well as professionally. Ultimately, you must decide if you want to commit the next five or six decades of your life to this profession.

CONCLUSION

This chapter has introduced you to the field of osteopathic medicine. As you go on to Chapter 2, the information presented here will be expanded, and you will read about the roots of osteopathic medicine and how it has emerged in the past fifty years as an important branch of medicine. The kinds of work that doctors of osteopathic medicine do in various places of employment will be highlighted. In Chapter 3, there is special emphasis on the areas in which osteopathic medicine differs from traditional or allopathic medicine in the treatment of medical problems. Chapter 4 will discuss what it takes to become a doctor of osteopathic medicine; you will learn about the terms of both educational and personal requirements. Chapter 5 will focus on what happens to doctors of osteopathic medicine after they finish osteopathic college, and Chapter 6 will examine what the future holds for the profession and how to get started. You will definitely want to spend some time carefully looking through the appendixes to learn about where you can get more information: on-line, in books, and from associations. These will help you learn everything you need to know about what it would be like to have a career as a doctor of osteopathic medicine.

Throughout this book you will enjoy reading about the actual life experiences of doctors of osteopathic medicine and about their careers. You will be able to decide if this is truly a vocation that you wish to pursue further.

CHAPTER 2

THE ROOTS
OF THE PROFESSION

Osteopathic medicine has made tremendous strides in recent years, most notably in the current number of practicing D.O.s, but the roots of osteopathic medicine go back at least a hundred years. In fact, to understand the origins of osteopathic medicine, or osteopathy, as it was known for many years, you must look at the historic beginnings of medicine in colonial America. Between the establishment of the first American colony at Jamestown in 1607 and the first American college of medicine in Philadelphia in 1765 was a period of 158 years.

During that period, medical practice was fractured and only as good as the physician you were seeing. There were some physicians who had obtained a formal medical background in European schools, but they were few. They also were considered the elite in medicine at that time and usually practiced among the upper classes. More numerous by far were the barber surgeons, apothecaries—as pharmacists of the time were known—and lay practitioners (those without any formal training in medicine).

In England, physicians received their training by apprenticeship. Many did continue their studies by earning their degrees at universities. These were the "gentlemen and scholars" of the profession. They did not work with their hands (as did the surgeons) or engage in trade (as did the apothecaries).

Surgeons learned their skills through apprenticeship. Although they treated people of all classes, their social status was considered beneath that of the physician. Apothecaries also were trained by apprenticeship and sometimes in hospitals. Since they made their living through the sale of drugs, they often were tempted to prescribe them heavily, earning them a reputation as "hard-dosing islanders."

COLONIAL MEDICINE

In the colonies, these distinctions tended to blur and the townspeople sought medical aid from the best person available. Especially on the frontier, but also in the more established communities, clergymen often were consulted on medical issues. For example, the Reverend Cotton Mather, a prominent clergyman and Massachusetts colonist, at one point felt strongly enough to recommend inoculation for smallpox, over the objections of the only doctor in Boston.

Another prominent person in the medical world of the period was the midwife, who was a standard part of the medical scene. But since regulation was not known or practiced, almost anyone could practice medicine and did, whether their skills came from bits of medical lore passed on by relatives and friends, or from knowledge of one special cure for a given disease or ailment.

With conditions for medical practice in such turmoil, practitioners usually had to turn to some other business to sustain them. People tended to be their own doctors and turned to medical aid as a last resort. The doctor's success, therefore, depended more on the degree of confidence he inspired rather than on any formal education. Such confidence on the part of the practitioner's patients might be based on published or oral credentials. In the most frequent cases, it might be the result of skills obtained through experience or from some special talent or from divine inspiration.

In England, medical apprenticeships usually ran for seven years; in America, during the colonial period, the apprenticeship was closer to three or four years. However, even this was not certain, for as one observer commented, in nine out of ten cases, the apprenticeship was little more than "the registry of the student's name in the doctor's office."

The First Medical School

The year 1765 was a pivotal one for medical practice in the colonies, for it was the year that the first medical school in the colonies was founded in Philadelphia. By 1800, there were ten medical schools in the new nation, all in the East. Since the faculties of these schools tended to be European university graduates, there was much criticism of the apprenticeship system and of the doctor, who at the same time wished to be physician, surgeon, apothecary, and dentist. Such practitioners were considered frauds, because the training at the medical schools of the day was aimed at turning out physicians who were skilled not only in medicine but who were gentlemen able to read Latin, Greek, or French. These doctors also were students who understood mathematics and the sciences.

The graduates of these pioneering medical schools were barely able to serve the growing population of the nation, since their numbers were so few and it was difficult to establish a practice because of wars. There also was the competition of untrained practitioners and shortages of textbooks and teaching materials to contend with.

Besides the more formal training of the medical schools described above, there were several other routes pursued in the practice of medicine, including quackery, folk and herbal healing, and those who followed the teachings of an unproved school of homeopathy. Some of this mixture of skills and abilities has been linked to the early nineteenth-century belief in the rights and abilities of the common man. All this made attempts at regulation almost impossible. Even so, the nineteenth century saw a tremendous growth in the number of medical schools—amidst the almost total lack of regulation by state and national legislative bodies.

During that period, very few of the medical schools were connected with universities, supervised by trustees, or run by paid faculty members. Most often, self-organized groups of practitioners would contact a college and seek to be authorized as the college's medical school. In most cases, the college would grant the group the right to set up the medical school because it offered the college a chance to expand. All it had to do was lend its name and prestige to the new medical school.

The medical school then operated as a proprietary or private medical college and often was not even on the campus of the main college or university. In time, many of these schools became legitimate university departments. Others evolved into independent medical schools. Some were sponsored by professional societies, but most were operated as independent proprietary schools.

INITIATING CHANGE

The educational programs offered at most of the early medical schools can hardly be considered on a par with the programs offered today, primarily because of lack of standards and the uneven quality of students entering these schools. At Harvard in 1869, the school's president, Charles Eliot, tried to establish written examinations for medical school graduation but was informed by the director of the medical school that "a majority of the students could hardly write." Other schools waived entrance and exit requirements in their competition for students.

At the end of the nineteenth century, the atmosphere of the medical schools was characterized by intense rivalry, short-term lectures, clinical demonstrations in large amphitheaters, and considerable profit to the schools. By the time of the landmark Flexner study of American medical education in 1910, there were some four hundred medical schools in operation, none of which were regulated. As a result of the study, sweeping changes were made in the curriculum and teaching method, which persist today.

Early efforts at regulation came through the professional societies, which at first attempted to limit the ability of unqualified graduates to sue for fees. Such efforts received some legislative support, but the advent of the Civil War saw most of these early efforts at regulation repealed.

The first effective reforms came between 1880 and 1910 with the development of state licensing boards. And the example of the excellent program at Johns Hopkins medical school and hospital set a standard of considerable influence. Finally, the publication of the Flexner study on the status of medical education in the United States in 1925 resulted in the closing of many poor and marginal medical schools.

A Pioneer in the Field

It was during this period of controversy in medical practice and education that Dr. Andrew Taylor Still first articulated his ideas in Kansas on how to improve the medical practice of his day. Dr. Still believed that the human body had much in common with a machine, which should function well if it is mechanically sound.

Dr. Still was a typical frontier doctor, having trained through apprenticeship with some medical lectures added later. As was common of frontier doctors of the period, he was involved in many other affairs besides the practice of medicine, including farming, mechanical work, and fighting in the Civil War as a captain in the medical corps of the Union Army from 1861 to 1864.

Dr. Andrew Taylor Still first enunciated the principles of osteopathy in 1874. He rejected the prevailing medicine of the time, especially its reliance on drugs and surgery.

When Dr. Still served as a Union physician during the Civil War, he became increasingly disillusioned with traditional medicine as it proved unable to stem the incidence of death and injury from poor sanitation and disease, which took a higher toll among soldiers, both northern and southern, than did bullets and other forms of weaponry. And while treating both settlers and Native Americans, Still faced the major epidemics of the time: smallpox, diphtheria, malaria, cholera, tuberculosis, and, of course, spinal meningitis.

At about the same time, Dr. Still could do nothing to prevent the deaths of three of his children from spinal meningitis. He became convinced that the reliance of doctors on medicine and drugs was completely wrong. In its place, he developed the osteopathic approach to medicine, which simply traced disturbances in the body's physiology to abnormalities in the musculoskeletal system. With the use of hands-on therapy to correct these structural abnormalities, he believed that physicians could strengthen the body's innate tendency to heal itself.

To many in the allopathic branch of medicine, Dr. Still's principles seemed to be lacking in fundamental correctness. For decades, the predominant medical branch, the allopathic profession, considered osteopathy outside the mainstream and dismissed the practitioners of this new form of medicine as cultists and fakes. Gradually, as osteopathy began to place greater emphasis on the use of drugs, surgery, and other therapies of mainstream medicine, it became more respectable, and indeed by the time the articles mentioned in Chapter 1 in *Medical Economics* appeared, the two branches of medicine had begun to patch up some of the differences that divided them.

TWO SCHOOLS OF MEDICINE

Shortly after the Civil War, there were two predominant schools of medicine: the allopathic, or medical doctor school, which is still predominant and is based on the theory of prescribing medicine that produces effects that differ from the disease treated, and the homeopathic school, which is founded on the belief that disease should be treated by giving small amounts of drugs that produce the symptoms of the disease in healthy people.

Dr. Still contended that the drugs and surgery of his day were either largely useless or actually poisons that added to the stress being placed on the already diseased body. Calomel, for example, used extensively to purge patients, contained a potentially deadly base of mercury. Dried foxglove, which contained digitalis, was widely used as a cure for heart ailments. However, it was often used in excessive amounts that made the problem worse.

Still's medical ideas stressed that the human body contained within it all that was necessary to maintain health, including all the substances required for good health, if they were properly stimulated. Central to his belief was the concept that the circulatory and nervous systems integrated the functions of the various body parts and systems. He believed that disorders of the musculoskeletal system could produce pressure on nerves and circulation, causing an abnormal response (disorder) in other organs of the body. He relied on his sense of touch to find such altered musculoskeletal conditions, such as areas of muscular tension or pressure points. To remedy the various bodily systems and organs involved, he applied pressure to the muscles or ligaments or skeletal functions and thereby eliminated the disease. The latter practice is the basis of osteopathic manipulation therapy today.

Even with the chaotic conditions that characterized medical practice of the time, Still's theories were considered radical, and when he attempted to present his ideas through the Baldwin and Baker University in Lawrence, Kansas, a school he and his family helped found, he was turned down without a hearing. Nor was he able to persuade the leaders of his own community to listen to his new medical philosophy.

ESTABLISHING A NEW SCHOOL

Traditional, or allopathic, medicine was in the mainstream, and Still's approach was definitely not. Even his own clergyman brother thought Still had lost his mind.

But Still persevered and became an itinerant doctor, moving around from community to community, first in Kansas and then in Missouri. He discussed his new concept with anyone who would listen. At first, he used some of the drugs that were then being prescribed. Eventually, however, he stopped administering drugs when he found he could get good results without them.

In time he was able to establish a solid practice in Kirksville, Missouri. Gradually he got busier, and people began to speak of his methods with great respect.

Eventually, it became obvious that there was a need for a school where osteopathic medicine could be taught. In

1892 the American School of Osteopathy, which eventually became the Kirksville College of Osteopathic Medicine, was chartered with an enrollment of seventeen students. The school's academic subjects, which were heavily grounded in anatomy and physiology, were taught by Dr. William Smith, a Scotsman who had studied medicine in Edinburgh and who had become interested in osteopathy in his travels in the United States. Dr. Still taught most of the clinical curriculum of osteopathic practice, both by lecture and demonstration and through actual practice with his own patients.

In succeeding years, both the number of students enrolled in the school and Dr. Still's own patient loads continued to increase. New buildings were erected, and the curricula became more extensive and better organized to include lectures in chemistry, histology, physics, toxicology, and pathology, among others.

By 1896 Dr. Still's school could boast 66 graduates, and new schools were organized in other parts of the country in 1896–97, bringing the total number of students enrolled in osteopathic medicine to 430. Yet more schools continued to be created.

However, by then the problem of licensing became a cause of contention with opposition to the licensing of doctors of osteopathic medicine developing in various states. A favorable court decision in Akron, Ohio, helped, but clearly there was need for legislative recognition of the new profession. This came with the passage of the first law licensing D.O.s in Vermont in 1896, while other efforts to obtain such licensure legislation were being made in Missouri and other states.

THE BIRTH OF THE ASSOCIATION

In 1897 a group in Kirksville organized the American Association for the Advancement of Osteopathy, and several months later, the Associated Colleges of Osteopathy was initiated. Ranking high on the agenda of both organizations were educational standards. The American Association for the Advancement of Osteopathy was later reorganized as the American Osteopathic Association in 1901, limiting membership to D.O.s from recognized schools.

Succeeding years saw the continued growth of the profession, legal recognition, launching of educational meetings, and the development of publications, as well as the construction of the first osteopathic hospitals.

Formal standards for the approval of osteopathic schools were adopted by the American Osteopathic Association in 1902, and the following year they were backed by on-site inspections. The standard course was increased from two to three years in 1905 and from three to four years in 1915, where it has remained over the years.

While the original charter of the American School of Osteopathy permitted the teaching of surgery, it apparently was not included in the school's early programs. However, by 1901 Still himself wrote that: "The osteopathic physician should be and is taught to do all operative surgery." By 1906 Still's school had its own hospital, where apparently Still himself did certain types of surgery, referring other types to surgeons who were more expert in them.

The ensuing years saw the further development of the profession, first with the formation of the American College of Osteopathic Surgeons in 1926 and then the American Osteopathic Hospital Association in 1934. Orthopedic surgeons organized themselves in 1941 and anesthesiologists in 1947.

Before 1911 there was an organization called the British Society of Osteopaths. In 1911 it changed its name to the British Osteopath Association (BOA). It became the formal arm of the American Osteopathic Association (AOA) for osteopaths trained "to uphold the professional ethical standards and to provide the public with a list of trained and qualified osteopaths, to advance osteopathy and to maintain a professional spirit." Members also were able to join the AOA. As with other associations, being a member was entirely up to the individual doctor.

A CHALLENGE TO THE PROFESSION

Preprofessional (undergraduate) entrance requirements for osteopathic college came earlier in some schools than in others. But by 1939, one year of preprofessional study was adopted as the requirement for osteopathic college admission. This was raised to two years in 1940, three in 1958, and today almost all colleges of osteopathic medicine require at least a bachelor's degree, and many entering students possess advanced degrees.

The growth of the profession continued slowly but steadily from the 1930s onward. The ease of licensing D.O.s in certain states made it more attractive for the doctor of osteopathic medicine to settle in those states than in others. As a result, the heaviest concentrations of doctors of osteopathic medicine developed in California, Michigan, Ohio, Pennsylvania, Missouri, Arizona, Florida, Texas, New Jersey, and New York.

In 1950 a landmark court decision in Audrain County, Missouri, established the right of a doctor of osteopathic medicine to practice in public hospitals as complete physicians in the full sense of the word.

At the same time, a long-standing fight for recognition of doctors of osteopathic medicine in the armed forces also came to a climax. Until that time, D.O.s had been drafted in two world wars, but they were not permitted to serve as medical officers. Now, because of legislation resulting from a hearing before the Armed Services Subcommittee in the U.S. Senate, doctors of osteopathic medicine were declared eligible for military commissions.

The campaign to end discrimination against doctors of osteopathic medicine sped up at midcentury. With all states now offering some form of legislative support for D.O.s, the goal shifted to obtaining full practice rights in all states. This goal was attained in 1973.

In 1961 the profession sustained what, at the time, seemed like a deathblow. This came about from an action resulting from several earlier rebuffs in the courts in California, which allowed the merger of the California Osteopathic Association with the California Medical Association. As part of the deal, the state's College of Osteopathic Physicians and Surgeons became a medical school. To make the deal complete, the state's twenty-five hundred doctors of osteopathic medicine were able to exchange their doctor of osteopathic medicine degrees for medical doctor degrees after attending a brief seminar and paying a $65 fee. A further prohibition prevented the licensing of any new doctor of osteopathic medicine in that state. For several years, as a result of this takeover, the prospects for osteopathic medicine looked bleak indeed, not only in California but throughout the country, where other such takeovers seemed to be a distinct possibility. The 1961 merger all but wiped out the California osteopathic community of the time. Worse still, the so-called "$65 M.D.s" as the

D.O.s were sarcastically referred to, were questionable in California when it came to hospital and academic appointments and virtually useless in other states for purposes of licensure.

The whole effort boomeranged against allopathic medicine, however, when no other states were prevailed upon to follow California's lead. And, wrote Dr. Norman Gevitz, one of the nation's most respected doctors of osteopathic medicine and a professor in the department of social medicine at Ohio University, as a result of the disastrous outcome of the California takeover, many undecided doctors of osteopathic medicine elsewhere in the country, who had adopted a wait and see attitude, decided they would prefer to remain doctors of osteopathic medicine.

That ended up being the turning point in the relations between the American Osteopathic Association and the medical establishment. Today osteopathic medicine is on the rise both as a method of treatment and in number of practitioners all over the country. There are now more than 43,500 doctors of osteopathic medicine in the United States, a 50 percent rise in the last decade alone. The profession has also made a dramatic comeback in California, where a 1971 court decision restored doctor of osteopathic medicine licensure. The state's 1,828 doctors of osteopathic medicine is one of the largest concentrations of D.O.s in any state, and it has two new schools of osteopathic medicine, as well.

GROWTH IN THE PROFESSION

In recent years, osteopathic medicine has made tremendous strides with the number of schools available for training having jumped from five in the late 1960s to nineteen today, and prospects for the launching of several new schools in the works. In addition, the number of osteopathic students is at an all-time high of nine thousand and the number of applicants is about ten thousand for twenty-five hundred spots, also a record high.

At a time when many contend that too many new doctors graduate each year from the nation's medical schools, osteopathic medicine continues to turn out new graduates at an accelerated pace. Its response to those who would seek to restrict the number of medical graduates is that there is a need for both allopathic and osteopathic primary care physicians. Most doctor of osteopathic medicine graduates practice primary care, including family practice, internal medicine, obstetrics and gynecology, and pediatrics. These are the frontline doctors, who are likely to see the patient first and who act as gatekeepers in referring patients to specialists when needed.

Osteopathy contends that nearly two-thirds of its graduates enter primary care, where the need for physicians is the greatest, as compared to about only a third in allopathic medicine. Although the profession accounts for less than 5 percent of the total number of physicians practicing today, it accounts for 10 percent of all primary care doctors. Then, too, say the leaders in the profession, doctors of osteopathic medicine are more likely to practice in smaller communities, those with populations of ten thousand or fewer.

Although relations between allopathic and osteopathic medicine have, for most of the 126-year history of osteopathy, often been bitter and contentious, with many medical doctors looking down on doctors of osteopathic medicine as fakers and quacks, these harsh days are largely bygone, and the relations between the two branches have probably never been better. A big step in building bridges between the two groups was taken by the American Medical Association in 1960, when for the first time it decided to accept doctors of osteopathic medicine as members. Today about eight thousand doctors of osteopathic medicine (nearly 20 percent of the total) belong to the AMA. In addition, it is not at all unusual to find medical doctors and doctors of osteopathic medicine practicing in the same groups. Doctors of osteopathic medicine have been allowed to join the medical staffs of many hospitals, which were formerly entirely controlled by M.D.s. The outlook is indeed good that relations between the two groups will not only continue to be positive, but will improve in the future.

CHAPTER 3

DOCTOR OF OSTEOPATHIC MEDICINE

To look at a doctor of osteopathic medicine in practice today—either in primary care or as a specialist—you would have to look very hard to spot any difference between the doctor of osteopathic medicine and his or her allopathic counterpart, the medical doctor. The similarities of the two professions are much greater than the differences. For example, both doctors of osteopathic medicine and medical doctors use all generally accepted diagnostic procedures, including x-rays and various other new imaging equipment, as well as laboratory analysis to detect health problems. And although osteopathic medicine stresses the body's natural ability to heal itself, D.O.s also prescribe medications, perform surgical procedures, and utilize other forms of therapy such as physical, occupational, and speech therapy, as valuable adjuncts to treating health problems.

While osteopathic physicians provide you with the best that medicine can offer, they can and do specialize in every recognizable medical area. These include more than twenty basic specialties and many other subspecialties, such as cardiology, neurology, and pulmonary medicine.

PROFILES OF SOME PRACTICING DOCTORS OF OSTEOPATHIC MEDICINE

Meet a Doctor of Osteopathic Medicine in Family Practice in Maryland

"I graduated from Kirksville College of Osteopathic Medicine, the school that was started by Dr. Still to train osteopathic physicians. I continued my education and received my bachelor's degree from Drew University in 1980. I chose the field of osteopathic medicine largely because it was in my family. Both my father and brother graduated from the Chicago College of Osteopathic Medicine and are currently practicing as doctors of osteopathic medicine.

"My Dad told me that of all the alumni of various osteopathic medical schools that he's encountered, those who had gone to Kirksville seemed to love that school the most and were the most supportive and proud of it.

"I was seeking to change my whole life and did not want to stay in New Jersey, where I'm from originally, any longer. Through a surgeon that my Dad knew, I was put in touch with a man at Kirksville College of Osteopathic Medicine, who is now my father-in-law. However, when I first met him, he was the president of the Kirksville Alumni Association.

"After listening to my story, he told me that he would help me if this were really what I wanted. I noticed that the people at Kirksville were all using their hands to give patients osteopathic manipulation, and they were proud of it. So I reapplied to osteopathic college and I was interviewed not only at Kirksville but at Kansas City and Chicago. I wound up at Kirksville because it was the first school, allopathic or osteopathic, that looked at me as a person.

"The curriculum at Kirksville was entirely different from allopathic medicine, where I did not touch a patient until the end of my second year of school. At Kirksville, the very first day, we touched each other and we broke that barrier. I have met many doctors of osteopathic medicine who really wanted to be medical doctors and felt that they settled for less in becoming doctors of osteopathic medicine. Others felt that there was sort of a stigma attached to being a D.O., especially from those in the allopathic medical community. And that's the way it used to be, but I am glad that I received the training in osteopathic manipulation and spent extra time training with people who were good with their hands.

"I found that the people at Kirksville were open to all so-called 'alternative' approaches to medicine, including acupuncture and chiropractic. Back East, I found many doctors of osteopathic medicine were interested in shedding their osteopathic training and practicing medicine just like a medical doctor. I realized, however, that in recent years, the trend toward medicine was changing. People were looking to a more holistic approach to health care. So when I did my family practice residency in Union, I was one of the few doctors there that continued to use my hands in osteopathic manipulative treatment.

"Today, whenever I can, whenever I think it is clinically appropriate, I use manipulative treatment. Obviously, osteopathic treatment is inappropriate for someone who comes in with a skin condition or similar ailment.

"If you look at the top five complaints in primary medicine, you will find they include headache, neck and back pain, and arthritis. So what is the best way of treating these complaints? In the new millennium are we going to rely on past practices of using more drugs and surgery and physical therapy for treating these patients, or will we find that patients are searching for something more efficacious in their treatment?

Today the trend among doctors of osteopathic medicine is to do more OMT in treating various illnesses. I learned how to help patients with colds and sinus problems from observing my father-in-law and how he practices. By using osteopathic techniques on my chest, he was helping to activate my immune system."

PRESIDENT HELPS DOCTORS
OF OSTEOPATHIC MEDICINE

"In 1993 my father-in-law and I treated former President Nixon. At that time my wife needed a special handicapped license, and we had to go to the chief of police, who was also a federal marshal for President Nixon. When I met with the chief of police to get my wife's handicapped privileges, I learned that he was also a security agent for former President Nixon and Republican Governor Nelson Rockefeller, both of whom used Dr. Kenneth Roland, D.O., of New York, as their personal physician. On the spur of the moment, I asked the chief of police if I could write to Nixon, offering him the services of me and my father-in-law if he should ever need a doctor of osteopathic medicine.

"About a year later I got a call from President Nixon's office advising that he had read my letter and wanted to come in. I was thunderstruck, and I immediately called my father-in-law on the phone. I advised President Nixon's office that we would be more than willing to fit him into our schedule.

"Nixon lived in Saddle River, which was close by, and we told him to use the side entrance when he came to avoid any fuss. About an hour later, a limousine pulled up and out came the president. Instead of using the discreet side entrance, he came right into the main waiting room, and we led him directly to my father-in-law, who worked on the president's neck for about a half hour or so. President Nixon told us that he used to travel around the world with a table handy for doing osteopathic manipulation treatments, given to him by Dr. Roland.

"In World War II, doctors of osteopathic medicine were not allowed to practice medicine. They were basically medics and that was it. Much of the primary care in World War II was done by D.O.s acting as medics. Nixon and Eisenhower were well aware of this, and their efforts helped to get doctors of osteopathic medicine licensed to practice medicine in all fifty states."

Meet a Doctor of Osteopathic Medicine in Family Practice in Michigan

"I am a graduate of the College of Osteopathic Medicine at Michigan State University, from which I received my Doctor of Osteopathic Medicine degree in 1981. I followed this by performing a residency in family practice at

Muskegon General Hospital, which at the time was an osteopathic hospital, although it is now both allopathic and osteopathic.

"There is a basic philosophical difference between osteopathic medicine and allopathic medicine. Let's just say that the osteopathic philosophy tends to be much more patient-centered rather than disease-centered. So as you are approaching patients with various clinical problems that present themselves to you, besides looking at the symptoms of a disease or ailment that may be a concern in treating that patient, you are, in osteopathic medicine, looking at how the disease affects the person and at his or her environment.

"A good example would be high blood pressure. You don't just toss medication at the patient. While prescribing medicine may be appropriate, there are also lifestyle changes to consider, including stresses in their family environment that greatly impact on the problem. Osteopathic physicians tend to look more at the entire picture, rather than simply focusing on the disease process.

"I have also heard it said of osteopathic and allopathic medicine that the science they practice is the same, but the art is different. It is a matter of following a person-centered approach, which we do in osteopathic medicine. This is explained by the fact that, historically, the colleges of osteopathic medicine recruited people who were interested in primary care disciplines and tended to be people-oriented.

That is why more doctors of osteopathic medicine are in primary care specialties than in other kinds of specialties.

"Currently, we are seeing a slight increase in the number of specialists in osteopathic medicine. Perhaps one reason why the primary care areas are becoming less attractive to those studying osteopathic medicine is because managed care has caused primary care disciplines in osteopathic medicine to suffer in their recruitment.

"I don't see a merger of the two branches of medicine in the future, even though relations between the two are perhaps better now than they have ever been. I don't think the osteopathic colleges would ever allow it, and most of the osteopathic physicians would resent it as well. While we are similar, we are a different breed of animal, and I don't think the osteopathic physicians would like being painted with the same brush as the medical doctors. While I practice with another doctor of osteopathic medicine in a partnership, we both have connections with allopathic doctors as well as osteopathic hospitals.

"Regarding osteopathic manipulative treatment, there are many days when we never use it, but it does affect how we approach a patient with musculoskeletal problems. This is not necessarily what one might consider osteopathic manipulative treatment. You don't have to perform OMT to use the knowledge base and the feeling that you have in assessing a patient's problems.

"We use osteopathic medical techniques frequently. We are more prone to placatory examinations on our patients. This is when we use our hands and examine the patients in a way that involves touch. You don't need to have been trained in osteopathic medicine techniques to evaluate a sprained ankle, but you do have to touch it. It's part of what we do, and we do this automatically; it's not an issue. You don't just look at the ankle; you move it to see how it functions."

CAREER ADVICE

"My advice to anyone who is seriously thinking about a career in osteopathic medicine is for you to keep in mind that osteopathic medicine is a rare mix of the ability to use people skills and science skills at the same time. Many physicians are skilled in the science aspect of medicine, but their people skills leave a lot to be desired. And in osteopathic medicine, you are expected to excel in both areas. If you are both a people-person and a skilled doctor, osteopathic medicine can be a very rewarding profession.

"I should mention that I decided to go into osteopathic medicine because I really wanted to go into primary care, and at that time, about twenty years ago, it was very unlikely that if I went into one of the allopathic programs I could become the kind of primary care doctor that I wanted to be. When I applied to Michigan State University, that was the first year that it even had a department of family practice, which was in 1976–77.

"It's probably different today. I think that most of those academic medical centers do have big departments of family practice now. I don't think that family practitioners are the low people on the totem pole, as was the case twenty years ago. Osteopathic medicine has surged in recent years because the public has told the medical profession that this is what it wants. Many people like osteopathic medicine's approach to health, and they are tired of having their ills treated as a disease process trapped in a body.

"I want to emphasize that our approach is not necessarily exclusive to osteopathic medicine, because you can certainly find an allopathic physician who practices with that same philosophy of treating the whole person and not the disease. Likewise, you can find an osteopath who is more concerned with disease and disease symptoms than in the entire range of problems surrounding that patient. The one statistic that all of the medical doctors and doctors of osteopathic medicine agree on is that 90 percent of doctors of osteopathic medicine—but only 10 percent of medical doctors—use that approach."

COMPLEMENTING MEDICAL SCIENCE—OMT

Doctors of osteopathic medicine complement their knowledge and use of medical science with the application of a hands-on diagnosis and treatment tool known as osteopathic manipulative treatment. Although not all doctors of osteopathic medicine use osteopathic manipulative therapy, (OMT), especially those in some of the more exotic specialties, such as radiology, pathology, or psychiatry, primary care physicians use osteopathic manipulative therapy on a good many of their patients and in treating a wide array of diseases and health problems.

Reasons for Using Osteopathic Manipulative Therapy

Doctors of osteopathic medicine use osteopathic manipulative therapy for several purposes: not merely to diagnose, but to treat and even prevent illness or injury. They may even use osteopathic manipulative therapy in conjunction with (or in place of) medication or surgery. That is only one difference—although it is perhaps the key difference—between the two branches of medicine.

Doctors of osteopathic medicine also like to emphasize that they take a whole person or holistic approach to health care. In this chapter you have read two interviews with doctors of osteopathic medicine who are practicing family medicine. However, as you continue reading this book, you will read many more interviews with doctors of osteopathic medicine who are currently practicing. These interviews will provide you with an in-depth picture of what it would be like if you chose to pursue a career in this field.

Instead of simply treating a disease or symptom, which is the approach emphasized by most medical doctors, as a doctor of osteopathic medicine you would be looking for the underlying causes of the disease. You would consider the general physical condition of the patient, plus the various mental and emotional factors in making your diagnosis.

Further, as a doctor of osteopathic medicine you would believe that all of the body's systems, including the musculoskeletal system, work together, and that disruptions or imbalances of one system may impair the function of another somewhere else in the body. As one doctor of osteopathic medicine put it: "We look at the musculoskeletal system as an entity unto itself in its influence on health and disease. You might compare it to your body, as the container, and the inside contents, as the inner workings of the body, and there's a relationship between the two in how the container influences the contents.

"It's like architecture and engineering put together—and the idea that structure and function work together. The architecture might be compared to the musculoskeletal system, and engineering to the body functions or systems. Osteopathic manipulation is applied anatomy and physiology."

Doctors of osteopathic medicine recognize that the body is capable of healing itself, though it constantly must fight physical, emotional, chemical, and nutritional "stressors" or causes of imbalance, to maintain good health. One thing further, osteopathic manipulative therapy is predicated upon your doctor of osteopathic medicine's knowledge of medicine. Once the D.O. has ruled out nonmechanical causes of injury or illness (through blood and urine testing, x-rays, imaging of the brain or of the stomach, colon and digestive system, among others) and based on what he or she finds, the doctor of osteopathic medicine may decide to use manipulation.

Osteopathic manipulative therapy is commonly used with various physical ailments such as lower back pain. This unique treatment, or modality, as doctors call it, also can be used by the D.O. to relieve the discomfort or musculoskeletal imbalance associated with a number of disorders, including asthma, carpal-tunnel disease, menstrual pain, migraines, and sinus disorders, to name a few.

TREATING THE PATIENT

Here is a typical scenario of how the doctor of osteopathic medicine works to cure your problem when you come in with a health complaint. Your physical exam will begin with an evaluation of your posture, spine, and balance. The D.O. will then use his or her fingers to palpate (examine by touch) your back, arms, and legs. He or she will check your joints for restriction of motion and/or pain during motion, as well as your muscles, tendons, and ligaments for tenderness, which can indicate a problem.

Once the physical exam is complete, your doctor of osteopathic medicine will put all of this information together with your medical history, as well as x-rays and other lab tests, and will then establish a treatment plan. Once the D.O. has eliminated nonmechanical causes for your problem, he or she may apply osteopathic manipulative therapy to your body's affected areas to remove restrictions and misalignments.

In short, osteopathic medicine is based on all the tools that medical science puts at the doctor's command, with osteopathic manipulative therapy added. This is strictly a resource of the doctor of osteopathic medicine, and it also places greater emphasis on touch or palpation as a tool of diagnosis.

Case Number One—Sara

Sara visits her doctor of osteopathic medicine complaining of a sharp pain in her side. Her physician asks her a series of questions about her pain, including what exactly it feels like when it hurts the most, and how long the pain lasts. They then discuss her medical history. The doctor of osteopathic medicine may order a series of lab tests to see if the pain is caused by disease of an organ—her gallbladder or appendix, for example. The tests show that this is not the case. Since Sara has indicated that she works in an office with a "surround style" desk, her doctor reasons that she may be suffering from postural/mechanical strain. Based on Sara's examination, her responses to the questions regarding her health, and the negative test results, her D.O. decides to use manipulation to relieve pain associated with motion and muscle strain caused by improper sitting and movement. Her doctor of osteopathic medicine also recommends changing the setup of her workstation to further relieve the pain.

Case Number Two—Jonathan

Jonathan's symptoms include cough, congestion, fever, and headache. Immediately suspecting chronic sinusitis, the doctor of osteopathic medicine conducts an exam and orders the appropriate tests. When the results confirm the diagnosis, the D.O. first prescribes an antibiotic to treat the infection; then he utilizes various osteopathic manipulative therapy techniques to promote drainage of the sinuses and relieve pain related to the infection. Jonathan's congestion and pain are lessoned after completing of two weeks of antibiotic therapy. Two weeks after that, his infection is cleared up.

Case Number Three—Jennifer

Jennifer credits osteopathic manipulative therapy with her lack of the back pain frequently encountered by pregnant women. The treatment takes fewer than five minutes and is part of Jennifer's regular checkup in her doctor's office. First the doctor has Jennifer lay on her left side on an examination table with her legs bent. She then kneads her muscles to stretch them and evaluates the condition of Jennifer's spine, checking for trouble spots. The D.O. realigns her spine, which makes a loud pop when it moves back into place.

Jennifer then switches sides and the process begins all over again. Jennifer's physician has been treating her with osteopathic manipulative therapy for about six months, since she started to complain about back pain. Partially out of curiosity, Jennifer agreed to give osteopathic manipulative therapy a try and is very happy with the results. Her doctor says, "OMT gives my patients a lot of back pain relief without medication." She has been using osteopathic manipulative therapy on pregnant women for five years. She goes on to say, "Though there are few medications you can't give to a pregnant patient, why prescribe a narcotic if it is not necessary?"

Osteopathic manipulative therapy can be done even after the woman is about sixteen weeks into her pregnancy. "You have to be creative," says Jennifer's D.O. "If a woman can't lay on her stomach, you can put her on her side or sit her in a chair. The treatment can be useful until delivery, not to mention afterwards. Patients even clamor for treatment after they deliver," says the doctor. "It makes them feel better."

SALARIES FOR DOCTORS
OF OSTEOPATHIC MEDICINE

Salaries for doctors of osteopathic medicine are comparable to those of medical doctors with some slight deviations. Salaries are based largely on several factors: where you choose to practice, the kind of practice you have— primary care or specialized—and the amount of experience you have. Generally, the highest salaries are to be found in the South and in the Midwest, with the lowest in the East and on the Pacific Coast. Specialty practices still pay far more than those in the primary care bracket, although earnings of specialists have risen at a much slower pace than in previous years, compared to the salaries of those in primary care.

Despite the effects of managed care, which have tended to depress the wages of physicians, since the emphasis is on wellness and prevention of illness, the American Medical Association revealed that the average doctor's salary in late 1998 increased to nearly $200,000 per year. This was net, after payment of expenses but before taxes. The increase in income, according to an article appearing in the *Chicago Sun-Times* in April 1998, showed that managed care had not caused the dramatic pay decreases predicted by doctors and the American Medical Association.

Salary Surveys

A similar survey of doctors' incomes in 1996 found that their earnings had declined to an average of $182,000, the first drop in more than a decade of American Medical Association record keeping.

At the same time, the survey showed that physicians' median net income rose from $160,000 in 1995 to $166,000 in 1996. (Median means that half the doctors surveyed earned more and half earned less.) Average earnings are higher because a minority of physicians—primarily in the specialties, such as neurosurgery or cardiac surgery—earned more than $300,000 a year.

Another survey, conducted by the Medical Group Management Association (MGMA) in 1998, revealed that salaries of doctors in primary care rose to a median of $139,244, while specialists' salaries jumped to $231,000. For primary care doctors, the increase was the highest since 1995. For specialists, the 1998 raise reverses a decline in 1997. Hospital-owned practices, which often guarantee income but lack practice-based auxiliary services that attract more revenue, lost almost $80,000 per physician, according to the MGMA.

Other Findings

- Dermatology (the study of the skin), with a 9.23 percent jump to a median income of $193,215, showed the largest salary leap of all specialties. Second was hematology (the study of the blood and blood producing organs)/ oncology (the study of tumors), up nearly 9 percent to $212,156.
- Pediatric/adolescent medicine showed the largest jump in primary care, up 2.43 percent to a median of $135,000. But internal medicine still led all primary care practice fields with $141,000 a year.

Another survey finding showed that specialists' salaries dipped greatly in multispecialty settings. Specialists in single-specialty groups earned a median of $299,000, but only $201,000 in multispecialty settings. Primary care doctors, on the other hand, showed salary increases of just the opposite. Primary care doctors' salaries showed a median of $137,700 in single-specialty settings, and $139,590 in multispecialty settings.

The number of hours a physician spends on-the-job in practice has decreased over the past few years. Physicians worked an average of fifty-six hours a week in 1997, down from fifty-seven hours a week in 1996. While the figure for hours worked showed a slight decline in 1997, the AMA notes that many doctors are actually working longer hours doing paperwork and authorizing medical procedures and referrals required under managed care contracts.

Although the number of hours in actual practice of medicine has decreased, D.O.s today expect to earn more than they did a few years ago. A survey conducted by the American Association of Colleges of Osteopathic Medicine in 1998 showed that graduating seniors expect to average $104,000 during their first year of practice, up 3.9 percent from 1997. Long-term income expectations (for those in practice for ten or more years) rose 3.3 percent to $190,000. Those choosing primary care careers expect much greater increases in earnings. Seniors planning to practice in the primary care field expect to earn $95,000, up 8.3 percent from 1996. Income expectations varied by sex and specialty choice, with expected first year earnings of women being 18 percent less than that of male seniors, and anticipated earnings from primary care careers being 16 percent less than nonprimary care.

The latest breakdown in earnings for various medical specialties was conducted by Physicians Search in 1997 and was compiled based on salary figures supplied by ten medical groups, ranging from the American Group Practice Association and the American Medical Association, to the Medical Group Management Association, Sullivan Cotter & Associates, and Physician Services of America. Salaries supplied by these various organizations were averaged to yield the following figures for various specialties. All figures are net, after expenses, but before taxes.

Specialty	*Annual Earnings*
Anesthesiology	$203,000
Cardiology	207,000
Emergency Medicine	157,000
Family Practice	122,000
General Surgery	190,000
Internal Medicine	127,000
Neurology	149,000
Obstetrics/Gynecology	204,000
Oncology	127,000

Pathology	175,000
Pediatrics	121,000
Psychiatry	130,000
Radiology	209,000

American Medical Survey

Residencies, which offer specialty training for osteopathic or medical doctor graduates, can last up to eight years and pay very little. The American Medical Survey showed that the median salary for residents in 1997 was about $36,000. This is very little compensation considering that residents are required to work an average of eighty to one hundred hours per week.

Fellowships for those training to pursue subspecialty careers such as fertility (a subspecialty of obstetrics/gynecology working with the reproductive system) or cardiology or neurology (subspecialties of internal medicine working with the heart and nervous system) can expect to earn a bit more than their general practice resident counterparts, anywhere from $30,000 to $40,000.

True, physicians have salaries among the highest of any occupation, but these figures have to be tempered by several other factors. For one, the training period that physicians are required to undergo before they can practice starts at eleven years and can be much longer. This includes four years of undergraduate college, four years of medical school, a year's internship (in the case of doctors of osteopathic medicine) and anywhere from three years to eight years for residency training, depending on the specialty pursued.

Tuition for osteopathic college is not inexpensive by any means, running anywhere from $9,000 per year for a public school to $21,500 per year for a private school. When you add fees, books and equipment, transportation, and room and board to this figure, the total comes to about $24,500 for a public school and $33,874 for a private school per year. Little wonder that the average senior finishing osteopathic college leaves with a debt of better than $105,000 representing loans from banks, the government, the student's own family, and friends. Many of these loans, especially those obtained from the government, call for repayment to begin when the student begins his or her residency.

In conclusion, the educational program is very long and intense if you decide to pursue a career as a doctor of osteopathic medicine. You will have many hours of study per day added to the time spent in college on various other studies. As a rule of thumb, you can figure about an hour of outside study per hour of classroom study or lecture. Medicine, regardless of whether it's osteopathic or allopathic, is really only for those with the greatest commitment to the field or who are most anxious to become physicians. It's a matter of survival of the fittest in medical school, and the years spent studying and in residency, when you have little or no income to show for your efforts, are long indeed, until you begin to practice. Only then will you see the fruits of your labors.

CHAPTER 4

GETTING INTO OSTEOPATHIC COLLEGE AND STAYING THERE

Getting into osteopathic college and staying there is not easy. As a rule, you can figure that there are four applicants for every available spot. This is more than the number for medical school: about three and a half applicants for every spot. Therefore, you can assume that your chances of being accepted into osteopathic school are about 25 to 33 percent, depending on the prestige and size of the school.

One of the reasons why this percentage is so low is the very high academic requirement to enter these schools. Although some schools will consider your application if you have as low as a 2.5 grade point average on a 4.0 grade point average (GPA) scale, the mean grade point average for all osteopathic students in 1997 was 3.5. Therefore, your chances of gaining admission with a GPA lower than 3.5 are slim. There is a possibility of being accepted with a lower GPA if you can show that your grades were substantially improved in the latter part of your college career.

Similarly, the requirements for the Medical College Admission Test that all would-be osteopathic medical students must take are also quite high: 8.63 for the biological sciences, 8.18 for the physical sciences, and 8.22 for verbal reasoning (out of a scale of 10).

Although admission requirements for osteopathic college call for only three years of undergraduate work (college) in most cases, you will need to have your bachelor's degree if you expect to be accepted. Why? Because the vast majority of those applying for osteopathic school admission have their bachelor's degree or a more advanced degree, so the majority of the people you're competing against will have the advantage of more education.

In addition, the curriculum is very difficult, especially for the first two years. They're often referred to as the basic science years, when you are expected to put in at least an hour of outside study for each hour of classroom or lecture work you complete.

MENTAL REQUIREMENTS FOR STUDENTS IN OSTEOPATHIC COLLEGE

Are you squeamish in the sight of blood or body functions? You should be prepared to witness some unpleasant or unnerving sights if you intend to enter this field.

How do you relate to other people? As a physician, especially a primary care physician, you must be able to get along well with all types of people. In addition, somewhere along the line, you will have to get used to the idea that you may experience the death of a patient. In some cases, no matter what you do for them or how hard you work to save them, this may not be possible. In addition, there is the very tough task of informing a patient that he or she will die. This can be especially difficult for many physicians, who may question what else they might have done to save a patient.

Finally, some patients who are sick may be disagreeable and may take out their frustrations and suffering on those who care for them in the hospital, especially the physician and the nurses. While this is not true of all patients, it is certainly a fact of life for any physician. What's more, there are patients who do not understand the pressures and hectic lives of their physicians. They may call you in the middle of the night and wake you up with complaints about a stomach pain or headache. These are circumstances that any physician will quickly confirm as part of his or her existence. Do you have the patience, the stamina, and the commitment to withstand this type of pressure?

If you are unsure of where you stand on these and similar questions, you might want to consider some other careers before making the financial, emotional, and time commitment required by medicine. In any event, you should consider taking a summer job as a hospital orderly transporting patients to various hospital departments, or as a volunteer, bringing patients their mail, and in some cases reading to them. Any kind of work that will bring you into contact with patients in a hospital or nursing home setting will help you to determine how well suited you are for the work.

Meet the Registrar at a Midwestern College of Osteopathic Medicine

"We have had people apply here who had a 4.0 grade point average but did not have the other qualifications that we are looking for in admission. For example, we are looking for a student who has a sincere desire to help people as shown in extracurricular and community activities, or someone who has demonstrated an awareness of the medical profession as shown by various medically related experiences.

"All applicants who can meet our entrance requirements then come in for an interview. This is a panel interview of three individuals including an osteopathic physician, a science faculty member, and a third- or fourth-year student.

"Interviewers do not have access to any of the student's academic accomplishments. They don't know what the grades or MCAT scores are, so they are primarily interested in finding out if the person can articulate why he or she is interested in osteopathic medicine, why he or she wants to be a doctor—things like that. Then each of the interviewers will independently make a recommendation. Their recommendations go to the admissions committee and the committee then makes its recommendations on each student to the Dean, who has the final approval.

"For the last few years there has been a considerable upsurge of interest in osteopathic medicine, and to a certain extent this can be explained by the increase in doctors of osteopathic medicine and by awareness on the part of the public. Currently we have nineteen osteopathic schools nationwide, and when people become educated about osteopathic medicine—when they realize what it is—they feel that the philosophy of osteopathic medicine more closely matches their own feelings about what medicine should be: the holistic approach, the viewing of the person as a whole instead of focusing on the disease. And they also like the concept that we start the clinical exposure to the patients very early in their training—in their first week of school—whereas in the allopathic program you may not come into contact with the patients until your third year of medical school. During the first year, our students learn how to do a physical examination right away. They actually have hands-on contact with the patient.

"There is no limit as to how many schools you can apply to. A few apply to all nineteen, but the average is about six or seven. I don't think that your chances of acceptance are increased any more by applying to a whole group of schools rather than to only a few. Of the schools that a student applies to, he or she may receive several acceptances. Then we receive a joint acceptance report, which shows what schools the student has been accepted by, so at a glance I can see if the student we have accepted has also been accepted at other osteopathic schools.

"We recommend that students apply for admission at the earliest possible date, and we start to accept applications as early as June 1 for the following year's study.

"To increase your chances of being accepted, you should plan on taking your MCAT examination in April and then completing your file as soon as possible. This would include sending in the supplementary application and two letters of recommendation—one of the letters has to be from a doctor of osteopathic medicine. Also, if you submit your file early on, your chances of acceptance are much better.

"We do look to how students answer the questions on the application; this can be a pretty good indicator as to their motivation to become osteopathic physicians, why they want to study osteopathic medicine, and what they can bring to their studies that would help them complete the program.

"My advice to those thinking of going to osteopathic college is to know all that they can about osteopathic medicine and to do some outside reading on health-care trends. Also I would recommend that they have a variety of exposure to health care.

"Actually, we emphasize primary care at this college, although it is close to Chicago with all of its medical centers and abundance of residencies available at various hospitals and medical centers. But we realize that there has to be some balance, so there will be some people who are admitted who want to be cardiologists or they know they want to go into surgery, and that's perfectly fine. But we just want to know what they are thinking about. And, of course, by the time students complete college, they may have changed their mind several times as to which way they want to go in osteopathic medicine. We may find, for example, a youngster who when he or she was admitted wanted to go into primary care, but after going through clinical rotations in the third or fourth years, he or she may decide to switch to radiology or neurology.

"In choosing a school, I would definitely encourage you to visit any of the schools in which you are interested and check out the location, facilities, faculty, and student body. When we bring people in for an interview, we realize that they are checking us out just like we are trying to get a fix on what makes them tick."

Meet a Second-Year Medical Student
in an Osteopathic College

"I am from the St. Louis area and completed my under-graduate work at the University of Missouri.

"After I finished college in 1980, I went to graduate school and obtained my Ph.D. in organic chemistry. I worked for several years for Amoco in its biotech division, doing work that interfaced between chemistry and biology and developing diagnostics. I became interested in medicine because many of the people to whom I reported were medical doctors, and I found their day-to-day jobs interesting. I spoke to a cousin of mine who went to osteopathic medical school, and because of what he told me about the profession, I decided to look into the field on my own. I found that there was a lot about osteopathic medicine that was very appealing to me. I liked the way D.O.s treat the entire body instead of focusing on specific symptoms and that there was not the emphasis on relying on prescriptions for medicine and drugs as a means of curing everything.

"Through speaking to several osteopathic physicians, one of the things that they impressed upon me was that in today's climate of HMOs, although the doctors of osteopathic medicine may not have recourse to osteopathic techniques as much as they might want to, they still develop a very strong appreciation for the relationship between the muscular and skeletal systems. As a result, we have a better understanding of the anatomy and the musculoskeletal system.

"I was accepted at several osteopathic schools, but my wife is from the Chicago area and she had a very good career here, and that was what determined that I come here to study. I think it was a good choice because this school has a rich history, and I talked with several graduates who spoke very highly of it. Attending this school seemed to be the perfect way to fill both my wife's needs and my own.

"Right now, I believe that I will enter internal medicine when I finish my training, though I realize that as I continue, I will be exposed to various other areas of medicine that I might find more appealing. One thing I know for sure is that there are several areas that I don't want to go into: surgery or pediatrics, for example, or OB/GYN.

"I am hardly typical of most students here, because I was working for almost five years after I finished grad school and before I entered this program. I am thirty-one years old but there are others who are older. Some osteopathic medical students have worked in other fields, many of them health related, before deciding to go to medical school. Most of my classmates are younger, but many of them have worked for a while or done research before applying to osteopathic medical school.

"Now that I have been here for a couple of years, I find that the work is more difficult than I thought it would be.

There's a lot of course work. Then when I come home from school, which is a long day in itself, I am ready to start my second job, which is to study what I learned in class.

"I have a baby son who acts like my alarm in waking me up! I'd say that 30 or 40 percent of my classmates are married. Very few of the students work, but some do. Some tutor other students for money, and I believe that we have one or two pharmacists who work part-time.

"In medical school, different subjects test different skills. For example, the skills that you use in anatomy are different from the ones that you use in biochemistry, and the skills that you use in osteopathic manipulation are different from those that you develop in pathology. In developing all of these various skills, you end up developing a broad knowledge base.

"Everything is challenging. I can't say that my second year of school is any easier than the first, but I feel more comfortable than I did in my first year. I don't feel the same anxiety about all of the unknowns, for example.

"I did consider allopathic as well as osteopathic schools when I decided to go into medicine—about five specific schools in each category. I was accepted at two osteopathic colleges, but at none of the allopathic schools. I don't feel at all that going to osteopathic school was indicative of a step down in my standards because the two branches are absolutely equivalent in terms of their skills levels and competency of students and faculty. I certainly don't feel that I am being short-changed or second-best or anything like that.

"As to finances, since osteopathic school is rather expensive, I accumulated quite a bit in my savings to cover the cost of tuition and other expenses. I have had to rely just a bit on student loans, which is really great.

"I have read in the *New England Journal of Medicine* that there has been a decline in the number of students applying to medical school. I am sure that a lot of this is due to the many years of study involved before you get your degree and become board certified in your specialty, as well as in the difficulty of the program itself. And this holds true of osteopathic medicine as well.

"So you are getting a lot of bright students who at one time might have considered medical school but are now going into all of these other areas: computers, business, and so forth. But for those students who are really interested in science and in helping others, I believe they would be very happy going into osteopathic medicine."

OTHER REQUIREMENTS FOR STUDENTS IN OSTEOPATHIC COLLEGE

In addition to the tough academic and study requirements, applicants for osteopathic college must meet certain visual, physical, and emotional requirements to take on the demanding schedule of studies and clinical work required of all osteopathic college students.

For the specific requirements, you can write to the registrar of the particular schools in which you are interested, or you can write to the Association of American Medical Colleges for the *College Information Booklet for the Osteopathic Profession.* This book lists the specific admission requirements for all of the osteopathic medical schools, as well as other valuable information.

Besides motivation and intellectual ability, there are many other requirements that you must meet to get into osteopathic college. While all osteopathic schools want applicants who have a broad, generalist background in the humanities, arts, and communications, they prefer that you have your bachelor's degree from an accredited college or university. Specific requirements call for at least six semester hours in English and eight semester hours each in the sciences: biology, chemistry, physics, and organic chemistry.

Math, though not required, will definitely prove helpful. In addition, most schools increasingly are looking for candidates who have taken courses in computer science and statistics. Also looked upon favorably are students who have taken honors courses and independent study or research.

As one admissions director put it: "We are not necessarily looking for the applicants with the strongest academic backgrounds. We are seeking students with strong academic credentials who have shown a sincere desire to help people as displayed in extracurricular and community activities. Also sought is the student who has shown an awareness of the medical profession as manifested by various medically related experiences."

There is one other big hurdle that you must overcome to gain admission to all osteopathic colleges, and that is to take and pass the MCAT (Medical College Admission Test) with reasonably good grades.

Given twice a year, in spring and in fall, this standardized exam tests you in four general areas: verbal reasoning, physical sciences, biological sciences, and writing ability. Schools prefer that you take the test early, in the spring, approximately eighteen months before you finish college. The test, running slightly less than six hours, is administered and scored by the American College Testing program (ACT). A manual describing the content and skills assessed is available at most college bookstores or can be purchased directly from the ACT.

The $150 fee for taking the test is sizable, but a fee reduction program is available to students pleading financial need by the American Association of Colleges of Osteopathic Medicine.

Also available from the ACT is a packet of materials for registration offering announcements, a registration card, and current information on dates, test locations, etc. It should be available from your health professions advisor.

The importance of this test cannot be overemphasized. All osteopathic schools rely heavily on the test results in evaluating your credentials. However, the MCAT is but one of the factors that schools look at in reviewing your background.

Once you have decided upon pursuing a career in osteopathic medicine, there remains the question of which school do you apply to. To help you decide, here are several factors to take into account:

- Do you prefer larger classes where lectures are stressed, or smaller classes allowing for more personal contact between you and the instructor? The few public osteopathic schools have larger lecture classes, which though more impersonal than the smaller classes do offer the opportunity of working together in smaller study groups.
- All osteopathic colleges stress primary care and are committed to exposing students to the various areas of primary care early on in their studies. At the same time, certain colleges, which are located in or near metropolitan areas, may offer more exposure and accessibility to

hospitals and clinics offering excellent training for those
who intend to specialize.

- Where do you wish to practice? Chances are that if you
want to work in a smaller community of say 100,000 or
fewer, your choice of a school in a smaller community
such as the Kirksville College of Osteopathic Medicine
in Missouri or the new Pikeville College of Osteopathic
Medicine in Kentucky, will prove more practical than
one located in a larger, urban area.
- What is your financial background? If money were a
problem, you would definitely be better off seeking entrance to a public school, where the tuition averages
$9,000 per year, compared with $21,500 per year for
private schools. In any event, you would definitely be
better off attending a school in your own state, public or
private, since state residents do receive a lower tuition in
either type of school. This undoubtedly explains why
more than 53 percent of all osteopathic students attend
schools in their own state.

Therefore, the requirements for getting into and finishing
osteopathic school are powerful indeed. However, there are
other equally compelling reasons to carefully consider if osteopathic school is for you, before you actually begin the admissions process.

Finally, there are years of internship and residency, at
least four years, and as many as seven or eight for some
specialties. During this period, you are expected to put in

an average of eighty to one hundred hours a week for wages that are low, approximately $35,000 per year, depending on your specialty.

COURSES YOU NEED TO PLAN ON TAKING

According to the University of Medicine and Dentistry of New Jersey (UMD) School of Osteopathic Medicine, in order to get your degree in osteopathic medicine, you would be required to take the following courses:

First Year

Gross Anatomy
Biochemistry
Histology
Microbiology
Neuroanatomy
Physiology

Second Year

Pathology
Pharmacology
Geriatrics

Pediatrics
Clinical Medicine
Behavioral Science

Third, Fourth, and Fifth Years

Clinical Years
Clinical Cases
Virtual Hospital
Osteopathy

OPPORTUNITIES FOR MINORITIES

Minority students—students considered to be underrepresented in the profession (black, Native American, and Hispanic)—enrolled in osteopathic medical schools in increasing numbers in 1997, with first-year enrollment of such underrepresented minorities increasing to 9.8 percent of all freshmen in 1997.

Is minority status or gender a factor in enrolling in osteopathic college? Not really. In fact, the growth rate among women has been much greater than that of men. In 1968, only 21 women were in the freshmen class. By 1997, more than 1,000 women had entered osteopathic medical schools, with an estimated 780 graduating in 1998. Women now make up more than 38 percent of the total enrollment in the nineteen schools of osteopathic medicine.

So being a woman or a member of a minority group should not be a stumbling block in applying to osteopathic school, nor should lack of funds, for as we will see below, funds are available if you have the intellectual goods and the motivation that are required to succeed in osteopathic medicine.

FINANCIAL COSTS OF ATTENDING OSTEOPATHIC COLLEGE

Cost is always an important consideration in selecting which osteopathic school you may want to attend. Osteopathic school tuition is expensive, even in the public colleges, if you are not a resident of the state in which the school is located.

As already noted, the tuition for osteopathic college is quite high for private schools and a little lower for public schools. When you add the cost of fees, room and board, and transportation, there is little wonder that the average osteopathic student's indebtedness, upon graduation, exceeded $100,000 in 1998 and is expected to rise in the future.

Financial Aid

Fortunately, help is available. Besides the funds that you might have been able to put together through jobs held before attending osteopathic college and money that your parents might provide, many loans and scholarships are available. You can also receive your share of financial aid from state and federal governments and from osteopathic sources. Last year, it was estimated that more than 92 percent of all freshman osteopathic students obtained some financial aid from the school they were attending. In fact, this is a very important consideration in applying to osteopathic college. It is to your benefit to check with the schools' financial aid departments to find out what loans, scholarships, grants, etc., are available and how much support you can expect to obtain from the various schools applied to.

LOANS

Last year, of the various sources of funds for osteopathic education, loans were by far the most important, supplying 76 percent of all funds available to freshmen. Scholarships were next in importance, accounting for 8 percent of all funds available. Parents supplied another 8 percent of funds available, and students' own savings accounted for 3 percent.

The federal government remains the major source of funding for loans borrowed directly by students. It should be noted that the federal Department of Education insures loans made by lenders to undergraduate and graduate students under Title IV of the Higher Education Act of 1965. For more information on available student aid, you can write for the American Association of Colleges of Osteopathic Medicine Application Service's *Financial Aid Handbook for Osteopathic Medical Students,* available at $10 per copy.

In 1998, the Stafford (formerly known as the Guaranteed Student Loan) program was the largest source of loans. About 93 percent of seniors had subsidized Stafford loans and 88 percent borrowed under the unsubsidized program. Other major sources of loans were the HEAL, NDSL, and SLS/PLUS programs.

Although no new funds are being granted under the HEAL program, it remains the most important source of funds for seniors in terms of the total amount borrowed, accounting for an average of $51,000 per senior. Since no new loans are available under this program, entering freshmen can expect to replace HEAL loans with unsubsidized Stafford loans and other sources.

Offering some encouragement to students seeking loans is the news that under Congressional Amendments to the Higher Education Act passed in 1998, the interest rate on many loans under the Stafford and SLS/PLUS programs will be lowered to 7.46 percent interest.

Besides loans to cover your tuition and other educational fees, you must also expect to cover personal expenses, such as room and board, transportation, and so forth. Such expenses averaged $7,200 for osteopathic seniors in 1998 and about $6,200 for freshmen that same year.

SCHOLARSHIPS

In addition, you can look to scholarships to provide a considerable amount of the funds that you will need to cover your expenses during your years in osteopathic school. About 36 percent of seniors had some scholarship funds during their four years in medical school. Such scholarships averaged $14,700 for seniors and $11,600 for other students.

There are a number of sources for such scholarships, such as the osteopathic schools themselves, which may have several scholarships available through charitably minded individuals, foundations, corporations, and so forth. Other scholarships are limited to students of a certain ethnic, religious, or racial background, or from a given community or state. There are literally dozens of such scholarships available. Although it may take some legwork on your part to find these scholarships, the effort will be well worth it since you may find that you qualify for one or more of them.

OTHER SOURCES

Obviously, if you can count on your parents for a certain amount of financial support, this will substantially cut down the amount of funds that you will have to obtain from other sources. However, if you are independent and must make your own way, then obviously you will incur more debt in financing your osteopathic education.

The type of school in which you enroll—that is, private or public—has a big effect on the amount of debt that you incur, because state subsidies to public schools help to reduce the cost to the students. However, thirteen of the nineteen osteopathic schools were privately owned, as compared with only six public schools. Because of this, 76 percent of all freshmen students registered at privately owned schools in 1997.

PREPARING FOR YOUR INTERVIEWS

If, after considering the pros and cons, you decide that osteopathic medicine offers the kind of career satisfaction you are seeking, your first step is to apply to the American Association of Colleges of Osteopathic Medicine Application Service, otherwise known as AACOMAS, a subsidiary of the American Association of Colleges of Osteopathic Medicine. This centralized service processes the transcripts and other forms you submit and allows you to file a single application form that can then be duplicated and sent to as many schools as you wish to apply to. Students ordinarily will send out an average of six applications each, but a few students will apply to all nineteen schools. According to several osteopathic school registrars, your chances of acceptance will not improve by applying to all nineteen schools than they will by applying to only six.

Early registration, by December for the following year, with AACOMAS is desirable, though you have until February of the year in which you seek to enroll to send in your credentials.

Ordinarily, the school to which you apply will then send you a supplemental application, after it reviews your AACOMAS application, to make sure that you meet the minimum requirements for admission. You then must complete the supplemental application and send it back with two letters of reference: one from a D.O. who knows you and another from one of your college professors.

The next step is being asked in for an interview. In 1999 in one large Midwest school, 3,486 applications were received. Of these 323 applicants, or 9 percent, were invited for interviews. In addition, of this group of applicants, 160 were accepted, roughly 50 percent of those who interviewed. This does not mean that your chances of being accepted by that school were only one in twenty. Bear in mind that each student averages six applications to various schools, which means that of the 3,486 applications received, only about 600 were bona fide applicants, which made your chances of being accepted by that school 1 in 3.5.

Most schools follow what is termed a rolling admissions process. Here your application and those of other applicants are reviewed regularly during the admissions period. Interviews are conducted and students are accepted until all of the classes are filled. Ordinarily, you would be notified of your selection status within two to four weeks of your interview date.

Once you agree to come in for an interview, several other applicants in a meeting with a three-person interview panel will join you. No one on the interview panel will have any information on your academic background, grade point average, and so forth. Then the team members will question you about your personal or professional aspirations, why you want to become a doctor, what makes you think you would be a good doctor, and so forth. The panel then rates you and the other students being interviewed.

After the interviews are finished, the team members forward their recommendations on each student. They can recommend that you be accepted, denied, or placed on an alternate list for possible acceptance later on. This recommendation is then sent to the dean for final approval. Ordinarily the interview process begins in September and ends in February of the year in which you wish to enroll.

EVALUATING OSTEOPATHIC COLLEGES

Of further note was the evaluation the graduating seniors gave the training they received in osteopathic medical school. For instance, in one recent year 24 percent of the seniors rated the quality of the training received as "very satisfied," 60 percent as "satisfied," 11 percent as neither "satisfactory" nor "unsatisfactory," and only 5 percent as "dissatisfied." As to mastery of clinical skills, 82 percent said they either were "confident" or "very confident" of their mastery of clinical skills.

Seniors also were asked to evaluate various areas of instruction as "appropriate," "inadequate," or "excessive." Topping the list of instructional areas with an "appropriate" rating of 88 percent was "screening for diseases," and "physician/patient relationship," closely followed by "basic medical science" with an 87 percent rating as "appropriate." At the bottom of the list were several areas that have gotten low marks as instructional areas for several years: "research techniques," "practice management," and "medical socio-economics."

In evaluating various instruction areas, many students called for more structured training in the clinical years. Some student comments related to the need for more time devoted to literature analysis and review and more continuity of OMT training throughout the four years of osteopathic school.

CHAPTER 5

AFTER OSTEOPATHIC
MEDICAL SCHOOL

ARE YOU READY TO PRACTICE?

Okay, you're finished with medical school, and you know what specialty you are interested in and where you want to practice. All that remains is to pass the licensure examination in your state and you are ready to set up your practice, right? Not quite, because the first step you have to take after completing medical school is to enter a twelve-month rotating internship. This must then be followed up with choosing a residency, which can last from one to seven years. In some cases, such as with cardiology and neurology, subspecialties of internal medicine, you may have to train for an additional two to three years on what is called a fellowship.

All states, the District of Columbia, and U.S. territories require that you be licensed as a physician before you can practice medicine, either osteopathic or allopathic. To be licensed as an osteopathic physician, you must first be a graduate of an accredited osteopathic medical school, pass a licensing examination, and have one to seven years of graduate medical education or more, if you want to practice a subspecialty such as cardiology.

You must then pass your state licensing examination and complete one to seven years or more of residency (specialty training). Usually, if you are licensed as a physician in one state, other states will grant you reciprocity, which means that your license will be valid there as well. This depends entirely on the individual state. In some states, you may have to pass that state's licensing exam to practice, even though you are licensed elsewhere.

Now that you are licensed, you are ready to practice, right? Not quite. You still have one more hurdle to pass and that is board certification. Most doctors of osteopathic medicine are seeking board certification, which is a notice that you have passed all the requirements to be certified in a given medical specialty. In order to become board certified, you are required to have from one to seven years or more of residency training. After finishing your residency, you must then pass a final examination for board certification by either the Accrediting Council on Graduate Medical

Education (ACGME) or the American Osteopathic Association (AOA). About half of the graduates of osteopathic colleges enter allopathic residencies while the other half enter osteopathic residencies. You can be certified by either AOA or ACGME, depending on the kind of residency you pursue, allopathic or osteopathic. There are approximately twenty-four specialty boards (the number keeps changing almost every year), ranging from allergy to immunology, each with their own particular requirements. In order to find out the requirements that apply to a given specialty, you should write to that specialty board or to the AOA or the ACGME.

NEARING THE FINISH LINE

Now let's take a detailed look at what happens after you finish osteopathic medical school. As noted above, the first step is to complete a one-year internship, which is intended to give you more exposure to various medical specialties in which you may be interested.

In 1998, as is usual, most graduating osteopathic school seniors (42 percent) planned to enter traditional rotating internships, while 14 percent were planning a specialty track program for which the internship counts as the first year of residency. Another 22 percent of the seniors were planning rotating residencies with special emphasis in other fields, such as emergency medicine, family practice, otolaryngology (eye, nose, and throat), pediatrics, and psychiatry. Finally, another 22 percent of all graduating seniors, nearly all planning to take an allopathic residency, were not planning an internship of any kind.

As to residencies, the percentage of senior osteopathic school graduates planning to take an AOA-approved residency has remained around 40 percent since 1990. Those planning an allopathic residency, that is, a residency program approved by the Accrediting Council on Graduate Medical Education (ACGME) remained at about 39 percent. There were an additional 11 percent or so of all graduating seniors who were planning residencies that had dual approval by both the AOA and ACGME, and finally there were approximately 10 percent who were planning residencies offered by the federal government, the military, or the Veterans Administration.

As to reasons for preferring an allopathic residency, about 55 percent of those planning such residencies replied that they were doing so because "they believe it offered better training." Another reason frequently cited for preferring an allopathic residency (cited by 50 percent of graduating seniors) was "a preferred osteopathic residency was not available in my geographic location." A good number of seniors (40 percent) said that an allopathic residency would "open more career opportunities." Other frequently offered reasons for preferring allopathic residencies were: "family considerations," "military or government obligations," "desire specialty training not available in osteopathic programs." In this regard, in 1999 a major emphasis of the AOA was the creation of additional residency programs for osteopathic students to increase the number of students choosing osteopathic residency training. This program will bear fruit over the next few years.

CAREER PLANS

Concering the career plans of osteopathic medical students, the greatest number of graduating seniors indicated that they were planning to enter group practice. Still others said they would prefer to be self-employed with a partner. Some said they would opt for private practice, and a few said they were planning to practice in an HMO or similar type of organization.

When asked what kind of practice these students intended to set up, 43 percent of the graduating seniors said they planned to practice as generalist or primary care doctors; 34 percent were planning to become specialists. Of those who chose primary care specialties (the more general and traditional osteopathic career choices), this was split among family practice, internal medicine, and pediatrics.

Family practice again led the pack in specialty choice, preferred by an estimated 27 percent of all seniors. This was followed by emergency medicine, chosen by 10 percent; internal medicine, 9 percent; pediatrics, 6 percent; OB/GYN, 5 percent. Approximately nineteen other specialties and subspecialties were also selected.

On a scale ranging from 0 (no influence) to 4 (major influence), seniors were asked to rate twelve possible factors that they felt had some influence on their specialty choices. Of these, "Intellectual Content" and "People Orientation," both with a 3.1 rating, were strong influences on those seniors choosing primary care specialties. Only "Intellectual Content" was rated by many choosing nonprimary care specialties as a major factor in their specialty choice. Of seniors planning primary care specialties, factors that were frequently cited as influencing their choices were skills required (rated 2.8 on the scale); lifestyle (predictable working hours, sufficient time for family) 2.7; role models (examples of physicians in the specialty) 2.6; desire for independence, 2.3; and academic environment, 2.0.

For seniors preferring nonprimary care specialties, besides intellectual content, leading factors in making their choice were skills required, 2.9; lifestyle, 2.5; role models, 2.4; and academic environment, 2.4.

Income expectations of all seniors rose moderately (3.3 percent) in 1998 from the previous year to $190,000 net, after ten years of practice. Income expectations varied by sex and specialty choice, with expected first-year practice earnings of women about 18 percent less than male seniors, and anticipated earnings from primary care specialties about 16 percent less than nonprimary care.

WHERE TO PRACTICE

New York continued as the leading state in terms of the planned practice location for seniors. As to other popular states in which to practice, Pennsylvania moved up a few places while Michigan and California dropped slightly, and Oklahoma moved into the top ten. Other popular choices of states in which to locate were Texas, Ohio, New Jersey, Florida, and Illinois. As might be expected, these are also the states that have the largest concentrations of doctors of osteopathic medicine in practice.

About 32 percent of the graduating seniors plan to locate their practices in major metropolitan areas (of 500,000 and more) while about 25 percent plan to practice in small towns (towns of fewer than 50,000) or in rural areas.

Of those going into major metropolitan areas, almost 42 percent plan to practice in medically underserved areas. A possible factor influencing the seniors' choice of the size of the town in which to practice was the size of their own hometowns. Of this connection, 31 percent indicated that they came from hometowns of 500,000 or more population, while 56 percent came from hometowns of 100,000 or fewer.

DIFFERENT KINDS OF PRACTICE

How do you know, specifically, what type of practice to choose, what specialty to select, and where your practice should be located? Here are a few tips.

First, what kind of a practice do you want to have? While the information that follows applies to a group practice, it might also apply to a private practice or a partnership.

Many doctors completing their residencies concentrate on location. They think in terms of relocating to the Sun Belt, near the ocean or the mountains, or to a temperate or dry climate. But there are many additional important considerations, such as the standing of the group you are joining and their style of practice.

In evaluating the group's standing, check with the medical director of the local hospital and other doctors in the community. Does the group have a good reputation? Have any of the doctors in the group been before the state licensing board for medical infractions?

If you are satisfied that the group is respectable, you should also check to see if you will fit in with their method of practice. For example, you may be considering joining a group of six pediatricians. You find out that the members of the group all play golf every Saturday morning, but you don't know how to play golf. Either you learn how to play quickly or you should strongly consider not joining the group, because you might not fit in.

In another case, one recruiter tells of a candidate who was considering joining a five-doctor practice in internal medicine and found out that each doctor was earning close to $300,000 a year. In order to accomplish this, they each slept in their offices at night so they would be up early and ready to practice the following morning. Such a setup would probably rule out 99 percent of those who were considering joining the practice.

What else should you consider before choosing a particular practice? For one, find out how many patients each doctor in the practice typically sees. Sure, you want to be busy, but you don't want to see so many patients a day that you feel like you are working on a factory assembly line and you aren't able to provide the quality care they deserve.

If you are considering joining a family practice group, will you be able to deliver babies? Perhaps 30 percent of all family practitioners do deliver babies, but they are located primarily in small towns. If you are considering an orthopedic group practice, will you be assigned to handle only office-based, nonsurgical cases, or will you be involved in the more serious cases calling for hospital surgery?

In terms of location, how do you decide where to establish your practice, assuming that it's a new practice, or where would you ideally like to practice? Surveys show education (where your children can attend school) as the leading determinate and housing as the second most important consideration. You should also consider whether or not housing in the area is affordable. Sure Los Angeles, San Francisco, Honolulu all sound ideal, but they also happen to be situated in very high-cost housing areas.

Ranking third in the doctors' list of priorities for settling on a location is security. How safe is the area to live and work in? Is it a good area in which to raise children? The fourth factor in determining location is recreation. This includes sports, parks, entertainment, and other choices. These are the factors that you should consider in determining where you want to practice—not the glamour of the location.

Meet a Doctor of Internal Medicine Practicing in Arizona

In the words of a graduate of the University of Health Sciences, College of Osteopathic Medicine at Kansas City who received his Doctor of Osteopathic Medicine in 1981 and went on to get his board certification in internal medicine and geriatrics:

"I chose this career after working as the chief of the laboratory at an osteopathic hospital and seeing what great doctors of osteopathic medicine there were and their approach to the patient as a whole person. That's when I knew what I wanted to do.

"After finishing osteopathic school, I completed a rotating internship followed by a three-year residency in internal medicine, and I have been practicing in Mesa, just outside of Phoenix, ever since.

"I am in a group practice with three other doctors of osteopathic medicine. As a doctor of osteopathic medicine, I have not met with any problems on the part of either the patients or the other medical doctors. As a matter of fact, most of my patients come through referrals because they know that I am a doctor of osteopathic medicine. Word of mouth is the best advertising I can have.

"I believe that the increasing interest in osteopathic medicine is partly due to the fact that the doctor of osteopathic medicine is just the kind of doctor that patients are looking for. When I receive referrals from other patients, I am told that they are delighted that someone will take care of them as a whole person and will spend time with them."

Meet a Doctor of Internal Medicine Practicing
in a Suburb of Chicago

"I've been in practice now for eleven years specializing in internal medicine. I am a graduate of the Chicago College of Osteopathic Medicine and conducted my residency at Cook County Hospital in the city. It was a straight medical doctor residency, and then I went into practice. I am also on the medical staffs of several local hospitals.

"Different doctors of osteopathic medicine have different approaches to manipulation. Some use it frequently in their treatment of patients. Basically, I approach medicine like any other internists. A big portion of my practice is devoted to patients with coronary disease, hypertension, and diabetes. It runs pretty much the gamut of what middle-aged and elderly patients have.

"My workload is the same as for other physicians. I work more than sixty hours a week. Actually, the time I spend seeing patients is about thirty to thirty-five hours per week, but I also have to check on my patients in the hospitals and I follow-up on them after they are released. I would say I put in sixty hours a week easily and work every other Saturday for half a day. In my present group, we take turns as to who is on call. That means every seventh week I am on call. That is one of the advantages of working in a large group. When I do have to be on call, I handle all phone calls and rounds on all of the hospitalized patients we have. This is to make sure that they are doing OK while they are in the hospital."

A TYPICAL DAY

"The day will depend on how many patients I have in the hospital, but it's rare that I don't have somebody in. For instance, this morning I was at one hospital at about 7:30 A.M. and saw my two patients there. I presently have no patients at the other two hospitals, but if I did, I'd have to see them as well. Sometimes, I start at 8:00 A.M. and am working toward earlier hours—so I see patients starting at 7:30 to 9:00 A.M. At noon everything shuts down for an hour for lunch. And then typically I'll see patients from about 1:00 to 5:00 P.M.

"We are also open Saturdays for half a day. I see patients about every fifteen to thirty minutes each in the office, and when patients call during the day, I receive about fifteen to twenty-five messages. I can complete a number of those callbacks during the day and then must take the rest of them home. When I get home, I do about a half-hour to an hour of paperwork. Last night at home, I called four people to talk over lab results and discuss other general questions. I spend additional time outside the office keeping up with my reading and going to seminars at hospitals.

"I don't have too many problems with patients or pressure at work. Maybe it's just a matter of time, but I've learned to become very comfortable with patients and in mapping out a treatment plan with them. That's my style. I don't dictate what I am going to have them do. I tell them what I think a patient with high blood pressure should do; either the patient is going to make changes in his or her lifestyle, lose weight, and watch salt intake, or he or she won't. In that case, I strongly press for the patient to get a blood pressure medicine, but I can't force anyone to do this."

SEEING A PATIENT

"Today in medicine patients come in to explain their problems or symptoms. I come up with a working theory as to the diagnosis and try to prove it as best I can. I try to avoid having them use expensive, high-tech treatments. Let's say that you come in with a headache. This can encompass anything from a simple muscle tension headache to a brain tumor. Should I order a CAT scan on every patient who comes in with a headache? I wouldn't be practicing good medicine if I were doing that indiscriminately.

"So I would conduct an examination, ask questions, look at the eyes, do a neurologic exam, and try to determine what kind of headache this person has and what's causing it. I would then review this with the patient and either start him or her on medication or suggest exercises, including stress reduction techniques and so forth.

"I do find I feel a lot of pressure from the business aspect of the practice and the frustrations of having to deal with managed care regulations. I work with a number of HMOs, and there are several models or kinds of HMOs. The most controlled type is where the patient is assigned a primary care doctor who acts as a gatekeeper. As such, you are supposed to prevent frivolous things from being ordered or done, but on the other hand, the gatekeeper is expected to deliver good medical care, treat the patient well, help the patient to live longer, and still follow HMO guidelines. And for this, the primary care doctor is awarded the grand sum of $7 to $10 per patient per month, and it gets to be very frustrating! If you dealt only with one HMO, it would not be so bad, but in this group, we work with six HMOs, each with its own requirements and regulations. They are somewhat similar, but there are differences. There is also the service model, which is not as restrictive, but still requires referral approval to see people not connected with the HMO. Then you have the PPO, which is even less restrictive.

"We have one staff person who devotes her entire day to dealing with referrals and with insurance companies. To refer a patient to a specialist, you must get written referral and approval. Simple things may not require approval, but you have to know the requirements. If a patient calls me in the middle of the night, I say to him or her: "Let's go over your insurance. Have you HMO Illinois? Which hospital are you affiliated with? Where should I have you go?" If I send the patient to a hospital that he or she is not affiliated with, the patient may have to pay for the visit to the emergency room.

"This kind of red tape makes me angry and makes the practice of medicine seem almost sinful. I deal with it as best as I can, but I certainly don't have to like it.

"My final advice is that if you really think you are interested in becoming a doctor of osteopathic medicine, you should be aware that it is a more holistic approach—that it encompasses more than simply the use of manipulation. To be honest, if you want to be a plastic surgeon, there are more opportunities for you to obtain a residency for training as a specialist as a medical doctor than as a doctor of osteopathic medicine."

FINDING WHERE TO GO

"When I finished, there were thirteen D.O. schools and there weren't too many hospitals with doctors of osteopathic medicine residencies, so the number of slots to do specialized residencies were limited. Today there are a lot of schools and an even greater number of students, which is why the osteopathic association opened up residencies to enable students to do an M.D. controlled residency as well as doctor of osteopathic medical residencies. At the time I was considered somewhat of a renegade. In my class I believe there were only seven or ten of us who did M.D. residencies. Now it is more open for doctors of osteopathic medicine at hospitals that are smaller and simply do not have the programs for plastic surgeons or neurosurgeons. My friend, for instance, had to go to Scotland for a pediatric neurology residency. I don't think he could have gotten it here. General fields—surgery, internal medicine, pediatrics, OB/GYN, family practice—are wide open. In these areas you will have no problems whatever in finding a residency that suits you.

"What does it take to succeed in osteopathic medicine? The same qualities that make for success in any form of primary care medicine. First of all, you must like people. You have to be able to talk to people and to work with people to make it as a physician. You must have empathy and patience. You have to listen to an awful lot to be able to pull out some ideas that may help the patient. Sure you run into some crotchety patients. But you learn in time to accept this, and you know that you will not be able to please everyone.

"You don't have to be an absolute genius to become a physician. But you must know your limitations when a patient's needs are beyond the scope of your ability to help.

And you must try to get the patient involved in his or her own care. Some older patients cannot accept this. Most of the time, I sit down and try to point out the options. But if they insist that they want your guidance, then I tell them: 'Look, this is what I want you to do.'"

Meet a Doctor of Osteopathic Medicine Specializing in Gastroenterology

"I trained at the New York College of Osteopathic Medicine in Long Island, New York, from 1984 to 1988. This was followed by a year's internship at the Sun Coast Hospital in Largo, Florida.

"I was exposed to osteopathic medicine in college while I was a student at Emory University in Atlanta. I was a premed student and had signed up to do some volunteer work at a small hospital just outside of Atlanta called Doctors Hospital, working in their recovery room. I worked there for about six months and found out that this was an osteopathic hospital. This was my first exposure to the profession and I met a lot of D.O.s there, learned a little about osteopathic medicine, and was quite impressed with it. That's how it all started.

"It was not until I took a residency in internal medicine at Winthrop University Hospital in Mineola, New York, for three years that I started to think about gastroenterology, or GI as we call it in medicine, and then I did a fellowship in

GI for another three years at the University of Illinois in Chicago.

"One of the attractive aspects of osteopathic medicine, I felt, was the 'hands-on' type of approach that we practice, including osteopathic manipulation. I always enjoyed that part of the training. What I found was that in GI you not only got a chance to use your mind in trying to diagnose or treat a patient, but many of the procedures involve the use of the hands—not with regard to osteopathic manipulation, but they do involve the use of the hands. So I liked the cognitive or thinking aspect of the profession in combination with the hands-on approach that it afforded me, which I enjoy.

"The residency that I pursued at the University of Illinois happened to involve an allopathic program. The fact that I am a D.O. has helped in many respects. I do get referrals from other D.O.s who are in primary care—internists, family practitioners, and so forth. The osteopathic family is very tightly knit, so we work with each other to a greater extent than we would if it were an M.D. who was involved.

"There may have been some bumps in the road in the course of my training, but if so, I am unaware of it. There was always talk of the prejudice that many D.O.s had encountered in the past, while I was in medical school, and this was always in the back of my mind, but I have found that on a day-to-day basis, people will accept you for the physician that you are—D.O. or M.D.

"I am practicing in several north suburban hospitals and am well accepted on the medical staffs of all three. Currently I am active actually in only a few gastroenterology societies, which restrict their members to GI practitioners.

"As to lack or not of training facilities for specialists such as in my field of gastroenterology, I feel that the present emphasis on training of primary care physicians should always take priority in osteopathic medicine, because that is where the roots of the profession lie and have been since its founding by Dr. Still, back in 1874.

"If the profession continues to grow and can organize new fellowships for the training of specialists, fine. But it should not come at the cost of abandoning the emphasis on primary care. So I would like the present two-to-one ratio of primary care physicians to specialists to continue, for at least the foreseeable future.

"In my own case, I was considering applying for a fellowship in GI at a Chicago osteopathic hospital, but a larger program at the University of Illinois accepted me and I accepted it.

"While there will undoubtedly be more demand for specialty and subspecialty training in the profession in the future, I still would not like osteopathic medicine to lose sight of its main goal—the training of good primary care physicians.

"To accommodate the students who want to pursue specialties and subspecialties, students will undoubtedly have to continue to train in allopathic facilities, as has been the case in the past.

"I would certainly recommend that any student thinking of going into this profession should be exposed to it by volunteering as a high school or college student to work in an osteopathic hospital or to talk to D.O.s about the work. See what their feelings are and read all that you can about the profession. If you feel that the profession seems to be what you are looking for, then it would be right for you.

"I think that the training and curriculum of osteopathic medicine is the same as that of the M.D., but we have the bonus of practicing the osteopathic approach and emphasizing the oneness of the body with its function."

CHAPTER 6

LOOKING TO THE FUTURE

To get a sense of where osteopathic medicine is going and which are the hottest opportunities, we'll start out with a few general comments about the profession and follow with specifics about the most popular and lucrative areas of practice, or specialization.

EMPLOYMENT OPPORTUNITIES

To begin with, it's a virtual certainty that employment of osteopathic physicians will grow faster than average for all occupations through 2006, due to the continued growth of the profession. Here the number of aging people, which is increasing rapidly, will spur the overall growth in the number of physicians. New technology will make for more testing, which means there will be an even greater demand for physicians. Today, doctors can conduct more tests, perform more procedures, and treat conditions formerly considered untreatable. Job opportunities will be best for primary care

111

doctors, such as general and family practitioners, and internists, as well as pediatricians, obstetricians and gynecologists, geriatric specialists (those specializing in medical care of the elderly), and preventive care specialists.

Because of the growth of managed care programs, which now cover most citizens, fewer specialists will be in demand due to the efforts of such programs to control health costs and increase restrictions on testing and other medical services. But the number of specialists is still increasing. This is expected to create a competition in jobs among specialists, especially for those working in large cities or suburban areas, and for those working for hospitals, such as anesthesiologists and radiologists.

Several leading medical organizations, such as the Academy of Sciences Institute of Medicine and the Pew Health Professions Commission, have predicted an oversupply of physicians in general, especially among specialists. They suggest that steps be taken immediately to cut down the supply of physicians by curbing the number of residency spots available. However, leaders in the osteopathic profession question whether this should apply to osteopathic medicine, since most osteopathic physicians go into primary care or practice in smaller communities (those of fewer than 100,000), or both, where job opportunities are great. Even those osteopathic physicians who plan to practice in larger urban areas tend to practice in medically underserved communities, where the need is also great. Those osteopathic students who have specialized in nonprimary care areas, where the need is not as great, will nevertheless continue to have opportunities to practice because of the number of D.O.s who retire or otherwise leave the profession.

EARNINGS

As to the future of specific fields in osteopathic medicine, a recent survey by *Medical Economics* shows that earnings increased in the two big fields of primary care medicine, but dropped in the area of surgical specialities, showing that there may not be as great a need for specialists as there is for general practitioners.

If you were practicing as an internist in 1998, your net income rose to 6 percent of what the typical neurosurgeon earned last year. If you were a family practitioner, your median net earnings was about 52 percent of that reported for orthopedists (those who practice orthopedic surgery). While this may sound like a salary much lower than that of the orthopedist, it is still an improvement over salaries in 1997, when family practitioners' earnings were only 48 percent of those of orthopedists. Overall, surgical specialists showed a drop of 3.8 percent in net income. But family physicians' net earnings climbed 6.5 percent to $132,400. This was more than the $131,780 reported by internists.

A further brake on earnings is imposed by HMOs, where the rise in net earnings was reportedly zero, or none at all.

Of the sixteen fields analyzed in the survey, only four showed any gains at all, the largest being family practitioners. None of the surgical fields registered any gains in income. Of those participating in the survey, earnings declined or stayed flat in the nine census areas in urban, suburban, and rural communities. Practitioners in the inner cities reported sharp gains in net income. One reason for this might be because of the increased coverage in Medicaid under managed care. Even so, those participating in HMOs showed an increase of $33,150 more in earnings than those who did not.

Earnings were highest in practices consisting of five to nine physicians, while four-doctor groups, previously first in the charts a year ago, are now third highest in net earnings per participant.

Where are the opportunities the best for practicing osteopathic physicians? By all accounts, the South is the most open job market for D.O.s. The median salary reported for all physicians throughout the South was $169,940 in the South Atlantic, $165,300 in the Mid-South, $174,000 in the Southwest. The area reporting the next highest earnings per doctor was the Midwest Great Lakes, where median physician salaries reported were $163,000, followed by the East where doctors' earnings were a median of $155,000. Lowest earnings reported were those from the West and the Pacific Coast areas, where the median income was $150,620. The key factor here is managed care, with its restrictions on testing and other medical services and hospital use, which has more influence on earnings on the West Coast than in other areas of the country.

In closing, it should be noted that while the earnings of doctors in the surgical specialties have flattened out or even declined in several cases, the earnings for many primary care specialists, particularly family practitioners, continued to rise for the last few years. What's more, the gap between what you can expect to earn as a specialist and as a primary care practitioner is shrinking and can be expected to continue to shrink for the next few years at least.

ACCREDITED SCHOOLS OF OSTEOPATHY

The following is a comprehensive list of accredited schools of osteopathy in the United States:

Arizona College of Osteopathic Medicine
    (AZCOM)
    19555 North 59th Avenue
    Glendale, AZ 85308
    (602) 572-3200

Chicago College of Osteopathic Medicine
    555 31st Street
    Downers Grove, IL 60515-1235
    (630) 969-4400

Kirksville College of Osteopathic Medicine
    (KCOM)
    800 West Jefferson Street
    Kirksville, MO 63501
    (816) 626-2121

Lake Erie College of Osteopathic Medicine
    (LECOM)
    1858 West Grandview Boulevard
    Erie, PA 16509
    (814) 866-6641

Michigan State University College of
    Osteopathic Medicine (MSU-COM)
    East Fee Hall
    East Lansing, MI 48824
    (517) 355-9611

New York College of Osteopathic Medicine
    (NYCOM)
    Wheatley Road, Box 170
    Old Westbury, NY 11568
    (516) 626-6900

Nova Southeastern University College of
    Osteopathic Medicine (NSUCOM)
    3200 South University Drive
    Fort Lauderdale, FL 33328
    (954) 262-1000

Ohio University College of Osteopathic
    Medicine (OUCOM)
    Grosvenor and Irvine Halls
    Athens, OH 45701
    (614) 593-2500

Oklahoma State University College of
    Osteopathic Medicine (OSU/COM)
    1111 West 17th Street
    Tulsa, OK 74107
    (918) 582-1972

Philadelphia College of Osteopathic Medicine
    (PCOM)
    4170 City Avenue
    Philadelphia, PA 19131
    (215) 871-1000

Pikeville College of Osteopathic Medicine
    (PCSOM)
    214 Sycamore Street
    Pikeville, KY 41501
    (606) 432-9640

San Francisco College of Osteopathic Medicine
    (SFCOM)
    1210 Scott Street
    San Francisco, CA 94115
    (415) 292-0407

The University of Health Sciences-College of
    Osteopathic Medicine (UHS-COM)
    2105 Independence Boulevard
    Kansas City, MO 64124
    (816) 283-2000

University of Medicine and Dentistry of New
Jersey School of Osteopathic Medicine
(UMDNJ-SOM)
One Medical Center Drive, Suite 312
Stratford, NJ 08084
(609) 566-6990

University of New England College of
Osteopathic Medicine (UNECOM)
11 Hills Beach Road
Biddeford, ME 04005
(207) 283-0171

University of North Texas Health Science
Center–Texas College of Osteopathic
Medicine (UNTHSC)
3500 Camp Bowie Boulevard
Fort Worth, TX 76107
(817) 735-2000

University of Osteopathic Medicine and Health
Sciences/College of Osteopathic Medicine
and Surgery (UOMHS/COMS)
3200 Grand Avenue
Des Moines, IA 50312
(515) 271-1400

West Virginia School of Osteopathic Medicine
    (WVSOM)
    400 North Lee Street
    Lewisburg, WV 24901
    (304) 645-6270

Western University of the Health Sciences,
    College of Osteopathic Medicine of the
    Pacific (WesternU/COMP)
    College Plaza
    Pomona, CA 91766-1889
    (909) 623-6116

TOP TEN MOST POPULAR INTERNET SITES FOR OSTEOPATHIC MEDICAL INFORMATION

1. www.aacom.org AACOM—American Association of Colleges of Osteopathic Medicine

A wonderful resource for osteopathic inquiries, this site includes a guide to colleges, news and legislative issues, and other links.

2. Student Osteopathic Medical Association (SOMA) www.osteopathicweb.com

Official site of the largest osteopathic medical student organization in the world with more than 5,500 members.

3. Kirksville College of Osteopathic Medicine
   www.kcom.edu

This is the homepage for the college where osteopathy was founded.

4. The Association of Military Osteopathic Physicians and Surgeons
   www.amops.org

This is the association's official website. It serves and represents osteopathic physicians in the uniformed services.

5. American Osteopathic College of Occupational and Preventive Medicine
   www.aocopm.org

This is an affiliate society of the American Osteopathic Association. This site contains board certification information and division-specific information.

6. OsteopathOnline.com
   www.osteopathonline.com

Includes a wealth of information for all those interested in the field, including the origins and future of the field, how to become an osteopath, and links to online journals and resources.

7. Student Doctor ™
   www.osteopathic.com

This is a helpful student resource site that includes educational and entertainment directories. It also provides useful osteopathic links and discussion groups.

8. Still Alive
   www.rscom.com/osteo/journal/intro.htm

This is an international electronic professional journal for osteopathic manipulative medicine and naturopathic medicine.

9. Osteopathic™ Webring
   www.osteopathicmedicine.org

Webring is designed to promote osteopathic medical education and increase web traffic of those sites promoting osteopathic excellence. There are currently 175 members of this webring.

10. The British Osteopathic Association
    www.osteopathy.org

This site contains general information about osteopathy medicine in the United Kingdom with tips on back care, fact sheets, online ordering of leaflets, FAQs, and additional links.

RECOMMENDED READING

Use these books as sources of additional information.

American College of Mechano Therapy Staff. *Textbook of Osteopathy.* Reprint edition. Pomeroy, WA: Health Research, 1996.

Ashmore, E. F. *Osteopathic Mechanics: A Textbook.* New York: Gordon Pr., 1991.

Ashmore, Edythe F. *Osteopathic Mechanics.* Pomeroy, WA: Health Research, 1996.

Barral, Jean Pierre and Pierre Mercier. *Visceral Manipulation.* Vista, CA: Eastland, 1988.

Belshaw, Chris, *Osteopathy: Is It for You?* Boston, MA: Element, 1993.

Collins, Frederick W. *Osteopathy.* Pomeroy, WA: Health Research, 1997.

Digiovanna, Eileen, L. (Editor) et al. *An Osteopathic Approach to Diagnosis and Treatment.* Philadelphia, PA: Lippincott-Raven, 1996.

Dorman, Thomas A. and Thomas Ravin. *Diagnosis and Injection Techniques in Orthopaedic Medicine.* Baltimore, MD: Williams & Wilkins, 1991.

Garrett, Stanley, X. *Osteopathy: Index of New Developments and Modern Research.* Washington, DC: ABBE Pubs. Assn., 1993.

Gevitz, Norman. *The D.O.s: Osteopathic Medicine in America.* Baltimore, MD: Johns Hopkins Press, 1991.

Greenman, Philip E. *Principles of Manual Medicine.* Baltimore, MD: Williams & Wilkins, 1989.

Johnston, William L. and Harry D. Friedman. *Functional Methods: A Manual for Palpatory Skill Development in Osteopathic Examination and Manipulation of Motor Function.* Indianapolis, IN: American Academy of Osteopathy, 1995.

Kain, Kathy L. and Jim Berns (Contributor). *Ortho-Bionomy: A Practical Manual.* Berkeley, CA: North Atlantic, 1997.

Kuchera, Michael and William Kuchera. *Osteopathic Considerations in Systemic Dysfunction.* Columbus, OH: Greyden Pr., 1996.

———. *Osteopathic Principles in Practice.* Columbus, OH: Greyden Pr., 1996.

Lederman, Eyal. *Fundamentals of Manual Therapy: Physiology, Neurology, and Psychology.* New York: Churchill, 1997.

McCabe, Donald Lee. *Handbook on Basic Clinical Manipulation.* Fort Myers, FL: Parthenon Pub., 1996.

Milne, Hugh. *The Heart of Listening: A Visionary Approach to Craniosacral Work.* Berkeley, CA: North Atlantic, 1998.

Seem, Mark A. *A New American Acupuncture: Acupuncture Osteopathy: The Myofascial Release of Bodymind's Holding Patterns.* Boulder, CO: Blue Poppy Pr., 1993.

Still, A. T. *Autobiography of Andrew T. Still with a History of the Discovery and Development of the Science of Osteopathy.* Reprint Edition. Medicine and Society in America.

———. *Osteopathy: Research and Practice.* Vista, CA: Eastland, 1992.

Triance, Edward. *Thorson's Introductory Guide to Osteopathy.*
    San Francisco: Thorsons, 1992.
Ward, Robert C. (Editor). *Foundations for Osteopathic Medicine.*
    Baltimore, MD: Williams & Wilkins, 1997.
Wischnitzer, Saul and Edith Wischnitzer. *Barron's Guide to
    Medical and Dental Schools,* 8th edition. Hauppauge, NY:
    Barron, 1997.

OSTEOPATHIC MEDICINE ASSOCIATIONS

NATIONAL ASSOCIATIONS

American Association of Colleges of
   Osteopathic Medicine
5550 Friendship Boulevard, Suite 310
Chevy Chase, MD 20815-7231

AACOM, the American Association of Colleges of Osteopathic Medicine, exists to lend support and assistance to the nation's osteopathic medical schools. The organization represents the administration, faculty, and students of all 19 medical schools in the United States.

It offers a centralized application service to assist students interested in enrolling in a college of osteopathic medicine.

American Osteopathic Association
  142 East Ontario Street
  Chicago, IL 60611

The American Osteopathic Association (AOA) was established to promote the public health, to encourage scientific research, and to maintain and improve high standards of medical education in osteopathic colleges.

American Osteopathic Healthcare Association
  5550 Friendship Boulevard, Suite 300
  Chevy Chase, MD 20815

Offers information about the AOHA mission and vision, osteopathic health-care systems membership and governance, osteopathic philosophy, member services, and related organizations.

SOMA: Student Osteopathic Medical
    Association

Provides information on SOMA, the officers, a directory of Internet links, and the *Student Doctor,* the official publication of SOMA.

STATE ASSOCIATIONS

Colorado Society of Osteopathic Medicine
Florida Osteopathic Medical Association

Montana Osteopathic Association
Pennsylvania Osteopathic Medical Association

AMERICAN OSTEOPATHIC ASSOCIATION
DIVISIONAL SOCIETIES

Alabama Osteopathic Medical Association
   Phone: (256) 356-9642
   Fax: (256) 447-9040

Alaska Osteopathic Medical Association
   Phone: (972) 417-1803
   Fax: (972) 417-1722

Arizona Osteopathic Medical Association
   Phone: (602) 266-6600
   Fax: (602) 266-1393

Arkansas Osteopathic Medical Association
   Phone: (501) 374-8900
   Fax: (501) 374-8959

Osteopathic Physicians and Surgeons of
   California
   Phone: (916) 561-0724
   Fax: (916) 561-0728

Colorado Society of Osteopathic Medicine
    Phone: (303) 322-1752
    Fax: (303) 322-1956

Connecticut Osteopathic Medical Society
    Phone: (860) 721-9900
    (800) 454-9663
    Fax: (860) 721-4403

Delaware State Osteopathic Medical Society
    Phone: (302) 529-2255
    Fax: (302) 529-2257

Osteopathic Association of the District of
    Columbia
    Phone: (703) 522-8404
    Fax: (703) 522-2692

Florida Osteopathic Medical Association
    Phone: (850) 878-7364
    Fax: (850) 942-7538

Georgia Osteopathic Medical Association
    Phone: (770) 493-9278
    Fax: (770) 908-3210

Hawaii Association of Osteopathic Physicians
    and Surgeons
    Phone: (808) 831-3000
    Fax: (808) 834-5763

Idaho Osteopathic Medical Association
    Phone: (208) 376-2522
    Fax: (208) 375-5860

Illinois Association of Osteopathic Physicians &
    Surgeons, Inc.
    Phone: (312) 202-8174
    Fax: (312) 202-8474

Indiana Osteopathic Association
    Phone: (317) 926-3009
    Fax: (317) 926-3984

Iowa Osteopathic Medical Association
    Phone: (515) 283-0002
    Fax: (515) 283-0355

Kansas Association of Osteopathic Medicine
    Phone: (913) 234-5563
    Fax: (913) 234-5564

Kentucky Osteopathic Medical Association
  Phone: (502) 223-5322
  Fax: (502) 223-4937

Louisiana Osteopathic Medical Association
  Phone: (318) 202-8190
  (800) 621-1773
  Fax: (318) 202-8490

Maine Osteopathic Association
  Phone: (297) 623-1101
  Fax: (201) 623-4228

Maryland Association of Osteopathic Physicians
  Phone: (410) 664-0621
  Fax: Same as phone number

Massachusetts Osteopathic Society, Inc.
  Phone: (800) 621-1773 Ext. 8190

Michigan Osteopathic Association
  Phone: (517) 347-1555
  Fax: (517) 347-1566

Association of Military Osteopathic Physicians
    & Surgeons
  Phone: (410) 519-8217
  Fax: (419) 519-7657

Minnesota Osteopathic Medical Society
 Phone: (612) 560-3346
 Fax: Same as phone number

Mississippi Osteopathic Medical Association
 Phone: (601) 366-0596
 Fax: (601) 234-5228

Missouri Association of Osteopathic Physicians
  & Surgeons, Inc.
 Phone: (573) 634-3415
 Fax: (573) 634-5635

Montana Osteopathic Association
 Phone: (406) 578-6177
 Fax: (406) 586-6740

Nevada Osteopathic Medical Association
 Phone: (702) 434-7112
 Fax: (702) 434-7110

New Hampshire Osteopathic Association, Inc.
 Phone: (603) 224-1901
 Fax: (603) 226-2432

New Jersey Association of Osteopathic
    Physicians & Surgeons
    Phone: (732) 940-9000
    Fax: (732) 940-8899

New Mexico Osteopathic Medical Association
    Phone: (505) 332-2146
    Fax: (505) 332-4861

New York State Osteopathic Medical Society,
    Inc.
    Phone: (315) 202-8175
    (800) 621-1773
    Fax: (315) 202-8474

North Carolina Osteopathic Medical Association
    Phone: (828) 698-4348
    Fax: (828) 698-4348

North Dakota State Osteopathic Association
    Phone: (701) 852-8798
    Fax: (701) 837-5410

Ohio Osteopathic Association
    Phone: (614) 299-2107
    Fax: (614) 294-0457

Oklahoma Osteopathic Association
  Phone: (405) 582-484
  Fax: (405) 528-6102

Osteopathic Physicians & Surgeons of Orgeon
  Phone: (503) 222-2779
  (800) 533-6776
  Fax: (503) 222-2392

Pennsylvania Osteopathic Medical Association
  Phone: (717) 939-9318
  Fax: (717) 939-7255

Rhode Island Society of Osteopathic Physicians
    & Surgeons
  Phone: (401) 721-9900
  (800) 454-9663
  Fax: (401) 721-4403

South Carolina Osteopathic Association
  Phone: (877) 886-3672

South Dakota Osteopathic Association
  Phone: (605) 347-3616
  Fax: (605) 347-4713

Tennessee Osteopathic Medical Association
    Phone: (615) 242-3032
    Fax: (615) 254-7047

Texas Osteopathic Medical Association
    Phone: (512) 708-8662
    (800) 444-8662
    Fax: (512) 708-1415

Utah Osteopathic Association
    Phone: (801) 798-0844
    Fax: (801) 794-1495

Vermont State Association of Osteopathic
        Physicians & Surgeons
    Phone: (802) 229-9418
    (800) 454-9663
    Fax: (802) 229-5619

Virginia Osteopathic Medical Association
    Phone: (703) 893-7269
    Fax: (703) 827-9703

Washington Osteopathic Medical Association,
        Inc.
    Phone: (206) 937-5358
    Fax: (206) 933-6529

West Virginia Society of Osteopathic Medicine,
    Inc.
  Phone: (304) 345-9836
  Fax: (304) 345-9865

Wisconsin Association of Osteopathic
    Physicians & Surgeons
  Phone: (262) 567-0520
  Fax: Same as phone number

Wyoming Association of Osteopathic Physicians
    & Surgeons
  Phone: (602) 266-5698
  (800) 842-0951
  Fax: (602) 266-5918

INTERNATIONAL OSTEOPATHIC ASSOCIATIONS

Osteopathic Association of Great Britain

The fundamental aims of the OAGB, as the United Kingdom's largest professional organization for osteopaths, will be to: Encourage teamwork and cooperation amongst its membership. Build a responsible and caring association of which osteopaths can truly be proud. Continually strive to develop and support beliefs and convictions that will guarantee the successful future of the osteopathic profession in that country.

International Academy of Osteopathy

Currently only written in the language of the Netherlands.

AMERICAN OSTEOPATHIC ASSOCIATION SPECIALTY AFFILIATES

American **Academy** of Osteopathy
3500 Depauw Boulevard, Suite 1080
Indianapolis, IN 46268-1136
Phone: (317) 879-1881
Fax: (317) 879-0563

American Osteopathic Academy of **Addiction
Medicine**
5550 Friendship Boulevard, Suite 300
Chevy Chase, MD 20815
Phone: (301) 968-4160
Fax: (301) 968-4199

American Osteopathic College of **Allergy &**
  Immunology
  3030 North Hayden Road, 26
  Scottsdale, AZ 85251
  Phone: (480) 585-1580
  Fax: (480) 585-1581

American Osteopathic College of
  Anesthesiologists
  17201 East U.S. Highway 40, No. 204
  Independence, MO 64055
  Phone: (816) 373-4700
  Fax: (816) 373-1529

American Osteopathic College of **Dermatology**
  P.O. Box 7525
  Kirksville, MO 63501-7525
  Phone: (660) 665-2184
  (800) 449-2623
  Fax: (660) 627-2623

American College of Osteopathic **Emergency**
  Physicians
  142 East Ontario Street, Suite 218
  Chicago, IL 60611-2818
  Phone: (312) 587-3709
  (800) 521-3709
  Fax: (312) 587-3713

American College of Osteopathic **Family
Physicians**
330 East Algonquin, Suite 1
Arlington Heights, IL 60005
Phone: (847) 818-1800
(800) 323-0794
Fax: (847) 228-9755

American College of Osteopathic **Internists**
5301 Wisconsin Avenue NW, Suite 670
Washington, DC 20015-2044
Phone: (301) 656-8877
(800) 323-5183
Fax: (302) 656-7133

American College of Osteopathic **Neurologists
& Psychiatrists**
Phone: (248) 553-0010 Ext. 295
Fax: (248) 553-0818

American College of Osteopathic **Obstetricians
& Gynecologists**
900 Auburn Road
Pontiac, MI 48342-3365
Phone: (248) 332-6360
Fax: (248) 332-4607

American Osteopathic College of **Occupational
& Preventive Medicine**
Phone: (949) 653-8694
Fax: (949) 654-0482

American College of Osteopathic Colleges of
**Ophthalmology & Otolaryngology Head
& Neck Surgery**
Phone: (937) 252-4958
(800) 455-9404
Fax: (937) 252-0968

American Osteopathic Academy of
Orthopedics
Phone: (954) 262-1700
(800) 741-2626

American College of Osteopathic **Pain
Management and Sclerotherapy**
Phone: (302) 996-0300
(800) 471-6114
Fax: (302) 996-5300

American Osteopathic College of **Pathologists**
Phone: (954) 432-9640

American College of Osteopathic **Pediatricians**
5550 Friendship Boulevard, Suite 300
Chevy Chase, MD 20815-7201
Phone: (301) 968-2642
Fax: (301) 968-4195

American Osteopathic College of **Proctology**
1020 Galloping Hill Road
Union, NJ 07083
Phone: (419) 251-6520
Fax: (419) 251-6854

American Osteopathic College of **Radiology**
119 East Second Street
Milan, MO 63556
Phone: (660) 265-4011
(800) 258-2627
Fax: (660) 265-3439

American Osteopathic College of
Rehabilitation Medicine
2214 Elmira Avenue
Des Plaines, IL 60018-2630
Phone: (847) 699-0048
Fax: (847) 296-1366

American Osteopathic College of
   Rheumatology, Inc.
   Phone: (732) 494-6688
   Fax: (732) 494-6689

American Osteopathic Academy of **Sports
   Medicine**
   7611 Elmwood Avenue, Suite 201
   Middleton, WI 53562
   Phone: (608) 831-4400
   Fax: (608) 831-5122

American College of Osteopathic **Surgeons**
   123 North Henry Street
   Alexandria, VA 22314-2903
   Phone: (703) 684-0416
   Fax: (703) 684-3280